U0129833

VOCABULARY

# 考研英语

# 极简刷词

## 手册

Graduate English

徐西坤　编著

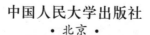

中国人民大学出版社
·北京·

# 前　言

## 一、考研，为什么必须背单词?

记得从业当初，面对很多不喜欢背单词的学生，我还给他们讲一些真实的或者虚构的通过英语学习走向人生巅峰的励志故事，以此来诱惑他们拿起自己的单词书去背诵一下。如果那些"鸡汤"能支撑他们背到 C 开头的单词，就算是成功了。渐渐地，我在苦口婆心地劝学生背单词的过程中，失去了一个培训老师应该有的耐心。现在，如果一个考研的学生问我："老师，我不想背单词怎么办?"我会毫不客气甚至有些生气地告诉他："你想考研，就必须背单词，不管你喜欢还是不喜欢，单词是必须要背的!"

那么，考研，为什么必须背单词? 我们来看 2019 年英语二阅读理解第 1 题:

**Researchers think that guilt can be a good thing because it may help_____.**

**[A] regulate a child's basic emotions**

**[B] improve a child's intellectual ability**

**[C] foster a child's moral development**

**[D] intensify a child's positive feelings**

如果不愿意背单词，那么像题干里的 guilt，选项中的 intellectual、foster、moral 和 intensify 这样的基础词汇，都会成为我们做题的障碍，必然影响我们做题的速度与质量。

我们再来看 2013 年英语一阅读理解第 36 题:

**Three provisions of Arizona's plan were overturned because they _____.**

**[A] overstepped the authority of federal immigration law**

**[B] disturbed the power balance between different states**

**[C] deprived the federal police of Constitutional powers**

**[D] contradicted both the federal and state policies**

如果不愿意背单词，我们又该如何面对题干里的 provisions、overturn，选项中的 overstep、authority、federal、disturb、deprive、Constitutional，还有那个 contradict?

显然，如果不背单词，我们在考场上甚至连看懂题干与选项的能力都没有，更别说信息量更大的原文。这个时候，无论是"××阅读法"还是"××阅读必杀技"都不能消除你无处安放的焦虑。能拯救你的，只有扎实的词汇量。

## 二、为什么还要弄一本"非主流"词汇手册？

很多同学可能不理解，市面上已经有太多销量很大的考研英语应试词汇书，那么，为什么还要再出一本这么薄的小册子？会不会"自取其辱"？虽然我出过很多其他考试用的词汇书，但我尚未涉及考研英语领域。我在休息之余，到书店翻阅在考生中广为流传的考研词汇书，发现一些问题，总结如下：

1. 这些书无论是按照字母正序排版还是乱序排版，基本上就是"单词＋派生词＋辅助记忆＋例句"这么一个套路。缺乏新意，选择的例句过难，读者无法通过例句体会单词的用法。我在课余时间和学生聊天得知，很多学生只看单词的汉语释义，其他内容基本上忽略。

2. 在选词方面，我感觉大多数词汇书没有很好地结合真题。有些书选择的单词过于简单，比如包括了 control、state、feel 这些中学词汇。而有的书选择单词时过于宽泛，毫无重点可言，甚至包括了很多与考研相关性不大的单词，比如 hen、barber、acrobat。考生花了大量的精力背诵一些对应试毫无用处的单词。（作为一个不拿书就可以讲阅读的老师，我深知哪些词有用，哪些词无用。）

3. 最大的问题，目前市面上几本销量不错的词汇书，均没有一个"练习"过程，考生只是机械地背诵单词，没有机会去训练单词，更没有机会去了解这些单词应该怎么运用到写作中。

## 三、《考研英语极简刷词手册》存在的理由是什么？

结合市面上词汇书的短板与自己的教学实践，我亲自编写的这本《考研英语极简词汇手册》，特点如下：

1. 单词分级："60＋词汇"与"80＋词汇"，针对不同目标的考生，比如一个考生底子薄弱，要求不高，过线就行，那么他必须掌握"60＋词汇"，可以不看"80＋词汇"。这样有的放矢，提高复习效率，可以把省下的时间用来复习其他科目。

2. 单词卡概念：根据考生实际需要，只保留单词的释义，而且这些释义经过严格的挑选，只保留对考试有用的部分。这是考生做题时最需要的东西。没有涉及搭配、用法、派生等内容。在排版上，单词与汉语释义分开，方便考生自测。

3. 配套练习：练习集中编排，以单词填空的形式，帮助学生巩固单词用法。题目整体难度不大，大多数改写自真题，可有效帮助考生在语境中巩固单词释义。许多句子还可以直接用于写作。背单词的同时提升写作语言的表达质感，一举两得。

4. 包含熟词僻义：考研英语中存在许多貌似简单的词汇，比如 fashion、address、stand、cap。实际上它们在考研中的考法一点都不简单：fashion "制定"；address "解决"；stand "忍受，经受"；cap "上限"。这本书收录了大量的这类词汇。

无论如何，作为一名从业 16 年的培训师，我希望考生能踏踏实实地背诵词汇，每天背 20 个，哪怕忘了 10 个，至少还收获了 10 个。通过不断地重复之前背诵的内容，我相信每位考生都能掌握这些核心考点词汇。英语学习，需要的是坚持与行动，无关天赋。

最后，祝每位考生能顺利进入自己梦想的研究生院深造学习。

徐西坤

**2024 年春**

# 目　录

## 第二部分 80+ 必备学术词汇 /31

## 第三部分　60+ 必备学术词汇配套练习 /51

## 第四部分　80+ 必备学术词汇配套练习 /111

# 附录 参考答案 /151

# 第一部分

## 60+必备学术词汇

### DAY 1 单词

apply [ə'plaɪ]

observe [əb'zɜ:v]

ceremony ['serəmənɪ]

recommend [ˌrekə'mend]

check [tʃek]

solve [sɒlv]

recognize ['rekəgnaɪz]

optimistic [ˌɒptɪ'mɪstɪk]

sensitive ['sensətɪv]

embarrass [ɪm'bærəs]

accompany [ə'kʌmpənɪ]

assist [ə'sɪst]

convey [kən'veɪ]

devote [dɪ'vəʊt]

mental ['mentl]

various ['veərɪəs]

stress [stres]

perform [pə'fɔ:m]

tendency ['tendənsɪ]

beneficial [ˌbenɪ'fɪʃl]

### DAY 2 单词

exact [ɪg'zækt]

account [ə'kaʊnt]

promote [prə'məʊt]

stand [stænd]

conduct [kən'dʌkt; 'kɒndʌkt]

recover [rɪ'kʌvə(r)]

deserve [dɪ'zɜ:v]

intend [ɪn'tend]

promise ['prɒmɪs]

classify ['klæsɪfaɪ]

exhibit [ɪg'zɪbɪt]

admire [əd'maɪə(r)]

accurate ['ækjərət]

object [əb'dʒekt; 'ɒbdʒɪkt]

contribute [kən'trɪbju:t]

expand [ɪk'spænd]

generation [ˌdʒenə'reɪʃn]

spiritual ['spɪrɪtʃʊəl]

talent ['tælənt]

technique [tek'ni:k]

# DAY 1 释义

| | |
|---|---|
| v. 申请，应用，使用 | v. 陪伴，伴奏 |
| v. 观察，**遵守** | v. 帮助，协助 |
| n. 典礼，仪式 | v. 表达，传递，运送 |
| v. 推荐，介绍 | v. 致力于，奉献于 |
| v. 检查，核对，**制止**　n. 支票 | adj. 精神的，脑力的 |
| v. 解决，溶解 | adj. 各种各样的 |
| v. 认出，识别，认可 | v. **强调**　n. 压力，紧张 |
| adj. 乐观的 | v. 执行，履行，表现，表演 |
| adj. 敏感的 | n. 倾向，趋势 |
| v. 使尴尬，使困惑 | adj. 有利的，有益的 |

# DAY 2 释义

| | |
|---|---|
| adj. 准确的，精确的 | v. 展览，显示　n. 展览品，展览会 |
| v. **解释，导致**　n. 账户，账目 | v. 钦佩，赞美 |
| v. 促进，推销，提升 | adj. 准确的 |
| v. 站立，**忍受，抵抗** | v. 反对　n. 物体，目标，**客体** |
| v. 组织，实施，进行，引导　n. 行为举止 | v. 有助于，贡献，捐赠 |
| v. 恢复，弥补 | v. 扩张，展开，膨胀 |
| v. 值得，应得 | n. 一代（人） |
| v. 打算，想要 | adj. 精神的，心灵的 |
| v. 承诺　n. 许诺 | n. 天才，才能 |
| v. 分类 | n. 技巧，技术 |

注：**加粗字体为特殊考法。下同。**

## DAY 3 单词

| | |
|---|---|
| achieve [ə'tʃi:v] | facility [fə'sɪləti] |
| afford [ə'fɔ:d] | anxious ['æŋkʃəs] |
| convince [kən'vɪns] | practical ['præktɪkl] |
| guarantee [ˌgærən'ti:] | essential [ɪ'senʃl] |
| inform [ɪn'fɔ:m] | accept [ək'sept] |
| refuse [rɪ'fju:z; 'refju:s] | bargain ['bɑ:gən] |
| despite [dɪ'spaɪt] | settle ['setl] |
| normal ['nɔ:ml] | claim [kleɪm] |
| prove [pru:v] | restore [rɪ'stɔ:(r)] |
| explore [ɪk'splɔ:(r)] | reduce [rɪ'dju:s] |

## DAY 4 单词

| | |
|---|---|
| offend [ə'fend] | chase [tʃeɪs] |
| puzzle ['pʌzl] | adapt [ə'dæpt] |
| admit [əd'mɪt] | compensate ['kɒmpenseɪt] |
| conflict [kən'flɪkt; 'kɒnflɪkt] | signal ['sɪgnəl] |
| curious ['kjʊərɪəs] | define [dɪ'faɪn] |
| guilty ['gɪltɪ] | create [krɪ'eɪt] |
| acquire [ə'kwaɪə(r)] | remind [rɪ'maɪnd] |
| comment ['kɒment] | origin ['ɒrɪdʒɪn] |
| raise [reɪz] | depend [dɪ'pend] |
| select [sɪ'lekt] | struggle ['strʌgl] |

# DAY 3 释义

| | |
|---|---|
| v. 获得，实现，成功 | n. 设施，设备，容易 |
| v. 买得起，提供 | adj. 焦虑的，**渴望的** |
| v. 说服，使信服 | adj. 实际的，实用的 |
| v. 保证，担保　n. 保证，保证人 | adj. 基本的，必要的 |
| v. 通知，告知 | v. 接受，承认 |
| v. 拒绝　n. 垃圾 | v. 讨价还价　n. 交易，便宜货 |
| n. **伤害**，**轻视**　prep. 即使，尽管 | v. 解决，定居 |
| adj. 正常的，标准的 | v. **宣称**，要求，**索取**　n. 声称 |
| v. 证明 | v. 恢复 |
| v. 探索，探测 | v. 减少，降低 |

# DAY 4 释义

| | |
|---|---|
| v. 冒犯，违反 | v. 追逐，追捕　n. 追逐 |
| v. 迷惑，使困惑　n. 谜 | v. 适应，改编 |
| v. 承认，允许进入 | v. 补偿，赔偿，**付报酬** |
| v. 冲突，矛盾　n. 冲突，矛盾 | v. 标志，表示　n. 信号 |
| adj. 好奇的 | v. 定义，明确 |
| adj. 有罪的，内疚的 | v. 创造，创作 |
| v. 获得，取得，学到 | v. 提醒，使提醒 |
| v. 发表评论　n. 评论 | n. 起源 |
| v. 提高，筹集，养育，引起 | v. 依赖，依靠，取决于 |
| v. 选择 | v. 奋斗，斗争　n. 斗争，冲突 |

## DAY 5 单词

| | |
|---|---|
| inspire [ɪnˈspaɪə(r)] | contact [ˈkɒntækt] |
| addition [əˈdɪʃn] | forgive [fəˈgɪv] |
| diverse [daɪˈvɜːs] | express [ɪkˈspres] |
| adjust [əˈdʒʌst] | tough [tʌf] |
| barrier [ˈbærɪə(r)] | aware [əˈweə(r)] |
| propose [prəˈpəʊz] | satisfy [ˈsætɪsfaɪ] |
| decline [dɪˈklaɪn] | abandon [əˈbændən] |
| impress [ɪmˈpres] | occasion [əˈkeɪʒn] |
| attract [əˈtrækt] | criticize [ˈkrɪtɪsaɪz] |
| concentrate [ˈkɒnsntreɪt] | gather [ˈgæðə(r)] |

## DAY 6 单词

| | |
|---|---|
| grateful [ˈgreɪtfl] | secure [sɪˈkjʊə(r)] |
| attempt [əˈtempt] | expense [ɪkˈspens] |
| purchase [ˈpɜːtʃəs] | adopt [əˈdɒpt] |
| exist [ɪgˈzɪst] | exhaust [ɪgˈzɔːst] |
| confuse [kənˈfjuːz] | apparent [əˈpærənt] |
| entertain [ˌentəˈteɪn] | frustrate [frʌˈstreɪt] |
| available [əˈveɪləbl] | commercial [kəˈmɜːʃl] |
| immediate [ɪˈmiːdɪət] | relieve [rɪˈliːv] |
| charge [tʃɑːdʒ] | confirm [kənˈfɜːm] |
| sufficient [səˈfɪʃnt] | efficient [ɪˈfɪʃnt] |

# DAY 5 释义

| | |
|---|---|
| *v.* 激发，鼓舞，使产生灵感 | *v.* 接触，联系　*n.* 接触 |
| *n.* 添加，增加 | *v.* 原谅，**免除（债务）** |
| *adj.* 不同的，各种各样的 | *v.* 表达　*n.* 快车，快递 |
| *v.* 调整，（使）适应 | *adj.* 艰苦的，艰难的，坚强的 |
| *n.* 障碍物，屏障 | *adj.* 意识到的 |
| *v.* 提议，建议，求婚 | *v.* 满足，使人满意 |
| *v.* 下降，衰退，**谢绝**　*n.* 下降，衰退 | *v.* 抛弃，遗弃，**放纵** |
| *v.* 给人留下印象 | *n.* 时机，场合 |
| *v.* 吸引 | *v.* 批评，评论 |
| *v.* 集中，全神贯注 | *v.* 收集，聚集 |

# DAY 6 释义

| | |
|---|---|
| *adj.* 感激的 | *v.* **保护，得到**　*adj.* 安全的，无虑的 |
| *v.* 试图，尝试　*n.* 试图，尝试 | *n.* 花费，代价 |
| *v.* 购买，获得　*n.* 购买 | *v.* 采取，采纳，收养 |
| *v.* 存在，生存 | *v.* 使筋疲力尽，**耗尽**　*n.* 废气 |
| *v.* 使混乱，使困惑 | *adj.* 明显的 |
| *v.* 娱乐，招待 | *v.* 挫败，受挫 |
| *adj.* 可获得的，有空的 | *n.* **商业广告**　*adj.* 商业的 |
| *adj.* 立刻的，直接的 | *v.* 减轻，减缓 |
| *v.* 充电，指责，索费　*n.* 费用，掌管，控告 | *v.* 确认，证实 |
| *adj.* 足够的，充分的 | *adj.* 有效率的 |

# DAY 7 单词

| | |
|---|---|
| sympathy ['sɪmpəθɪ] | require [rɪ'kwaɪə(r)] |
| stubborn ['stʌbən] | constant ['kɒnstənt] |
| request [rɪ'kwest] | defend [dɪ'fend] |
| ignore [ɪg'nɔ:(r)] | imagine [ɪ'mædʒɪn] |
| predict [prɪ'dɪkt] | occasionally [ə'keɪʒnəli] |
| return [rɪ't3:n] | maintain [meɪn'teɪn] |
| approach [ə'prəʊtʃ] | associate [ə'səʊsɪeɪt; ə'səʊsɪət] |
| blind [blaɪnd] | delight [dɪ'laɪt] |
| reflect [rɪ'flekt] | wisdom ['wɪzdəm] |
| desperate ['despərət] | flexible ['fleksəbl] |

# DAY 8 单词

| | |
|---|---|
| persuade [pə'sweɪd] | reasonable ['ri:znəbl] |
| organize ['ɔ:gənaɪz] | cautious ['kɔ:ʃəs] |
| handle ['hændl] | disturb [dɪ'st3:b] |
| awaken [ə'weɪkən] | amaze [ə'meɪz] |
| replace [rɪ'pleɪs] | contrary ['kɒntrərɪ] |
| abundant [ə'bʌndənt] | voluntary ['vɒləntrɪ] |
| innocent ['ɪnəsnt] | primary ['praɪmərɪ] |
| shelter ['ʃeltə(r)] | fantastic [fæn'tæstɪk] |
| prohibit [prə'hɪbɪt] | occupy ['ɒkjʊpaɪ] |
| expose [ɪk'spəʊz] | accommodate [ə'kɒmədeɪt] |

# DAY 7 释义

| | |
|---|---|
| *n.* 同情，赞同 | *v.* 需要，要求 |
| *adj.* 顽固的，倔强的 | *adj.* 不变的，经常的 |
| *v.* 要求，请求　*n.* 要求 | *v.* 辩护，防护 |
| *v.* 忽视，不理睬 | *v.* 想象 |
| *v.* 预言，预测 | *adv.* 偶尔地 |
| *v.* 返回，恢复，**以……相报**　*n.* 返回，回报 | *v.* 维持，维修，**主张** |
| *v.* 走进，处理，接近　*n.* 方法，方式，接近 | *v.* 联想，联系，交往　*adj.* 联合的，副的 |
| *v.* 使失明，**使失去理智**　*adj.* 盲目的，瞎的 | *v.* (使)高兴　*n.* 高兴 |
| *v.* 反映，反射，表达，**反省** | *n.* 智慧，才智 |
| *adj.* 不顾一切的，绝望的，**极度渴望的** | *adj.* 灵活的，易弯曲的 |

# DAY 8 释义

| | |
|---|---|
| *v.* 说服，劝说，使某人相信 | *adj.* 合理的，公道的 |
| *v.* 组织 | *adj.* 谨慎的 |
| *v.* 处理，应对　*n.* 把手 | *v.* 打扰，妨碍 |
| *v.* 唤醒，唤起，使……意识到 | *v.* 使吃惊 |
| *v.* 取代，替代 | *n.* [the ~] 相反的事实(或情况)　*adj.* 相反的 |
| *adj.* 丰富的，充裕的 | |
| *adj.* 无辜的，无罪的，无知的 | *adj.* 自愿的，自发的 |
| *v.* **保护，躲避**　*n.* 庇护，避难所 | *adj.* 主要的，初级的，基本的 |
| *v.* 阻止，禁止 | *adj.* 奇异的，异想天开的，极好的 |
| *v.* 揭露，揭发，使曝光 | *v.* 占据，占领，居住，**使忙碌** |
| | *v.* 容纳，提供食宿，(使)适应 |

## DAY 9 单词

| | |
|---|---|
| elegant ['elɪɡənt] | regretful [rɪ'ɡretfl] |
| absorb [əb'zɔːb] | document ['dɒkjʊment; 'dɒkjʊmənt] |
| conventional [kən'venʃənl] | professional [prə'feʃənl] |
| scare [skeə(r)] | recycle [ˌriː'saɪkl] |
| process [prə'ses; 'prəʊses] | strengthen ['streŋθn] |
| conscious ['kɒnʃəs] | arouse [ə'raʊz] |
| affect [ə'fekt] | potential [pə'tenʃl] |
| interaction [ˌɪntər'ækʃn] | exploit [ɪk'splɔɪt; 'eksplɔɪt] |
| distinguish [dɪ'stɪŋgwɪʃ] | impact [ɪm'pækt; 'ɪmpækt] |
| celebrate ['selɪbreɪt] | formal ['fɔːml] |

## DAY 10 单词

| | |
|---|---|
| vital ['vaɪtl] | affirm [ə'fɜːm] |
| effective [ɪ'fektɪv] | sustain [sə'steɪn] |
| adequate ['ædɪkwət] | tolerate ['tɒləreɪt] |
| host [həʊst] | display [dɪ'spleɪ] |
| identify [aɪ'dentɪfaɪ] | remove [rɪ'muːv] |
| manufacture [ˌmænjʊ'fæktʃə(r)] | estimate ['estɪmeɪt; 'estɪmət] |
| resident ['rezɪdənt] | depress [dɪ'pres] |
| visible ['vɪzəbl] | stable ['steɪbl] |
| oppose [ə'pəʊz] | reject [rɪ'dʒekt] |
| establish [ɪ'stæblɪʃ] | generous ['dʒenərəs] |

# DAY 9 释义

| | |
|---|---|
| *adj.* 优雅的，**简洁的** | *adj.* 遗憾的，惋惜的 |
| *v.* 吸收，吸引 | *v.* **记录**　*n.* 文件 |
| *adj.* 传统的，惯例的 | *n.* 专业人员　*adj.* 专业的，职业的 |
| *v.* (使)害怕　*n.* 恐惧，大恐慌 | *v.* 回收利用，循环使用　*n.* 回收利用 |
| *v.* 加工，处理　*n.* 过程 | *v.* 增强，巩固 |
| *adj.* 意识到的 | *v.* 引起，唤醒，激发 |
| *v.* 影响，感动，**感染** | *n.* 潜能，可能性　*adj.* 潜在的，可能的 |
| *n.* 相互作用 | *v.* 开发，开拓，剥削　*n.* 功绩 |
| *v.* 区分，辨别 | *v.* **撞击**，影响　*n.* 影响，**碰撞** |
| *v.* 庆祝 | *adj.* 正式的，拘谨的 |

# DAY 10 释义

| | |
|---|---|
| *adj.* 至关重要的，生死攸关的 | *v.* 确认，肯定，证实 |
| *adj.* 有效的 | *v.* 维持，支撑，供养 |
| *adj.* 充足的，胜任的 | *v.* 忍受 |
| *v.* 主持，主办　*n.* 主人，**许多** | *v.* 显示，表现，陈列　*n.* 显示，炫耀 |
| *v.* 确定，识别，辨认出 | *v.* 迁移，开除，调动　*n.* 移动，搬家 |
| *v.* 制造，**捏造**　*n.* 制造，制造业 | *v.* 估计，估量　*n.* 估计，估价，判断，看法 |
| *n.* 居民　*adj.* 居住的 | *v.* 压抑，使沮丧，使萧条 |
| *adj.* 明显的，可见的 | *adj.* 稳定的，牢固的 |
| *v.* 反对 | *v.* 拒绝，排斥 |
| *v.* 建立，创立 | *adj.* 慷慨的，大方的 |

# DAY 11 单词

| | |
|---|---|
| announce [əˈnaʊns] | prejudice [ˈpredʒʊdɪs] |
| desirable [dɪˈzaɪərəbl] | distinct [dɪˈstɪŋkt] |
| standard [ˈstændəd] | addict [ˈædɪkt] |
| complex [ˈkɒmpleks] | indicate [ˈɪndɪkeɪt] |
| distribute [dɪˈstrɪbjuːt; ˈdɪstrɪbjuːt] | justify [ˈdʒʌstɪfaɪ] |
| exchange [ɪksˈtʃeɪndʒ] | expand [ɪkˈspænd] |
| gradually [ˈgrædʒʊəlɪ] | found [faʊnd] |
| novel [ˈnɒvl] | emerge [ɪˈmɜːdʒ] |
| overlook [ˌəʊvəˈlʊk] | respond [rɪˈspɒnd] |
| condemn [kənˈdem] | optional [ˈɒpʃənl] |

# DAY 12 单词

| | |
|---|---|
| fundamental [ˌfʌndəˈmentl] | release [rɪˈliːs] |
| triumph [ˈtraɪʌmf] | interrupt [ˌɪntəˈrʌpt] |
| represent [ˌreprɪˈzent] | neglect [nɪˈglekt] |
| burden [ˈbɜːdn] | consequence [ˈkɒnsɪkwəns] |
| regardless [rɪˈgɑːdləs] | academic [ˌækəˈdemɪk] |
| withdraw [wɪðˈdrɔː; wɪθˈdrɔː] | concept [ˈkɒnsept] |
| preserve [prɪˈzɜːv] | reliable [rɪˈlaɪəbl] |
| donate [dəʊˈneɪt] | deliver [dɪˈlɪvə(r)] |
| instant [ˈɪnstənt] | acknowledge [əkˈnɒlɪdʒ] |
| fluent [ˈfluːənt] | starve [stɑːv] |

# DAY 11 释义

| | |
|---|---|
| *v.* 宣布，通知 | *v.* **损害**，使有偏见　*n.* 偏见，**侵害** |
| *adj.* 可取的，令人向往的 | *adj.* 明显的，有区别的 |
| *n.* 标准　*adj.* 标准的 | *n.* 上瘾的人 |
| *n.* **综合设施**　*adj.* 复杂的 | *v.* 表明，预示 |
| *v.* 分发，分配，散布 | *v.* 证明……合理 |
| *v.* 交换，交易　*n.* 交换 | *v.* 扩张，发展 |
| *adv.* 逐渐地 | *v.* 创立，建立 |
| *n.* 小说　*adj.* **新颖的** | *v.* 出现，浮现 |
| *v.* 忽略，俯瞰，**宽恕，监督**　*n.* 忽视，眺望 | *v.* 回应，作出反应 |
| *v.* 谴责，指责 | *adj.* 可选择的 |

# DAY 12 释义

| | |
|---|---|
| *n.* 基本原理　*adj.* 基本的，根本的 | *v.* 释放，放开，公开　*n.* 释放，发布 |
| *v.* 获得胜利　*n.* 胜利 | *v.* 中断，打断，打扰　*n.* 中断 |
| *v.* 代表，描绘 | *v.* 忽略，忽视　*n.* 忽略，忽视 |
| *n.* 负担　*v.* 使担负(沉重的任务等) | *n.* 结果，**重要性** |
| *adj.* 不管的，不顾的　*adv.* 不管怎样 | *n.* 学者　*adj.* 学术的 |
| *v.* 撤退，收回，取钱 | *n.* 概念，观念 |
| *v.* 保存，保护　*n.* 保护区，**专门领域** | *adj.* 可靠的 |
| *v.* 捐赠，捐献 | *v.* 传送，履行，投递，发表 |
| *n.* 瞬间，立即　*adj.* 立即的，紧急的 | *v.* 承认，答谢 |
| *adj.* 流畅的，流利的 | *v.* 挨饿，**渴望** |

# DAY 13 单词

| | |
|---|---|
| motivate ['məʊtɪveɪt] | capacity [kə'pæsətɪ] |
| accelerate [ək'seləreɪt] | rural ['rʊərəl] |
| enormous [ɪ'nɔ:məs] | entitle [ɪn'taɪtl] |
| dedicate ['dedɪkeɪt] | debate [dɪ'beɪt] |
| productive [prə'dʌktɪv] | analyze ['ænəlaɪz] |
| recruit [rɪ'kru:t] | previous ['pri:vɪəs] |
| shortage ['ʃɔ:tɪdʒ] | moderate ['mɒdəreɪt; 'mɒdərət] |
| accomplish [ə'kʌmplɪʃ] | persist [pə'sɪst] |
| seize [si:z] | complicated ['kɒmplɪkeɪtɪd] |
| budget ['bʌdʒɪt] | objective [əb'dʒektɪv] |

# DAY 14 单词

| | |
|---|---|
| instruct [ɪn'strʌkt] | intelligent [ɪn'telɪdʒənt] |
| critical ['krɪtɪkl] | crisis ['kraɪsɪs] |
| survive [sə'vaɪv] | favorable ['feɪvərəbl] |
| assure [ə'ʃʊə(r); ə'ʃɔ:(r)] | appropriate [ə'prəʊprɪeɪt; ə'prəʊprɪət] |
| contrast [kən'trɑ:st; 'kɒntrɑ:st] | domestic [də'mestɪk] |
| moral ['mɒrəl] | construction [kən'strʌkʃn] |
| invest [ɪn'vest] | surface ['sɜ:fɪs] |
| temporary ['temprərɪ] | original [ə'rɪdʒənl] |
| considerable [kən'sɪdərəbl] | interpret [ɪn'tɜ:prɪt] |
| violate ['vaɪəleɪt] | arrange [ə'reɪndʒ] |

# DAY 13 释义

| | |
|---|---|
| v. 刺激，使有动机 | n. 能力，容量 |
| v. 加速，促进 | adj. 乡村的 |
| adj. 巨大的，庞大的 | v. 授权，使有资格 |
| v. 致力于，奉献于 | v. 辩论　n. 辩论 |
| adj. 多产的，有成效的 | v. 分析 |
| v. 征募，招募　n. 招聘，新成员 | adj. 以前的 |
| n. 缺乏，不足 | v. **节制，减轻**　adj. 温和的，有节制的 |
| v. 完成，实现 | v. 坚持，持续 |
| v. 抓住，理解 | adj. 复杂的 |
| v. 预算　n. 预算　adj. **廉价的** | n. 目标　adj. 客观的 |

# DAY 14 释义

| | |
|---|---|
| v. 指导，教授 | adj. 智能的，聪明的 |
| adj. 批评的，**关键的** | n. 危机，决定性时刻 |
| v. 幸存，存活 | adj. 有利的，赞成的 |
| v. 保证，使确信 | v. **占用**　adj. 适当的 |
| v. 对比，对照　n. 差异，对比 | adj. 国内的，家庭的，驯养的 |
| adj. 道德的 | n. 建设，建筑物 |
| v. 投资 | v. **浮出水面，显露**　n. 表面 |
| n. 临时工　adj. 临时的 | n. 原件，原版　adj. 原来的，首创的，新颖的 |
| adj. 相当大的，重要的 | v. 解释，解读，翻译 |
| v. 违反，侵犯 | v. 安排，排列，整理 |

# DAY 15 单词

| | |
|---|---|
| survey [sə'veɪ; 's3:veɪ] | capital ['kæpɪtl] |
| considerate [kən'sɪdərət] | emphasize ['emfəsaɪz] |
| enthusiastic [ɪn‚θju:zɪ'æstɪk] | obstacle ['ɒbstəkl] |
| harmony ['hɑ:mənɪ] | inflation [ɪn'fleɪʃn] |
| atmosphere ['ætməsfɪə(r)] | calculate ['kælkjʊleɪt] |
| threaten ['θretn] | indifferent [ɪn'dɪfrənt] |
| passive ['pæsɪv] | revenue ['revənju:] |
| appreciate [ə'pri:ʃɪeɪt] | artificial [‚ɑ:tɪ'fɪʃl] |
| capable ['keɪpəbl] | reproduce [‚ri:prə'dju:s] |
| circumstance ['s3:kəmstəns] | mutual ['mju:tʃʊəl] |

# DAY 16 单词

| | |
|---|---|
| proper ['prɒpə(r)] | track [træk] |
| religion [rɪ'lɪdʒən] | campaign [kæm'peɪn] |
| minimal ['mɪnɪml] | boost [bu:st] |
| quantity ['kwɒntətɪ] | fade [feɪd] |
| ensure [ɪn'ʃʊə(r); ɪn'ʃɔ:(r)] | equality [ɪ'kwɒlətɪ] |
| generate ['dʒenəreɪt] | tackle ['tækl] |
| trigger ['trɪgə(r)] | creative [krɪ'eɪtɪv] |
| credible ['kredəbl] | alarming [ə'lɑ:mɪŋ] |
| demonstrate ['demənstreɪt] | literate ['lɪtərət] |
| hesitate ['hezɪteɪt] | perspective [pə'spektɪv] |

# DAY 15 释义

| | |
|---|---|
| v. 调查，勘测　n. 调查，测量 | n. 首都，省会，**资金**　adj. 首都的，重要的 |
| adj. 体贴的，考虑周到的 | v. 强调，着重 |
| adj. 热情的，狂热的 | n. 障碍，干扰，妨碍 |
| n. 协调，和睦，融洽 | n. 膨胀，通货膨胀 |
| n. 气氛，大气，空气 | v. 计算，认为 |
| v. 威胁，恐吓 | adj. 冷淡的，中立的 |
| adj. 被动的，消极的 | n. 税收收入，财政收入 |
| v. 欣赏，感激，领会，**增值** | adj. 人造的，仿造的，虚伪的 |
| adj. 有能力的，有才干的 | v. 复制，再生，生殖 |
| n. 环境，状况 | adj. 共同的，相互的 |

# DAY 16 释义

| | |
|---|---|
| adj. 适当的 | v. 追踪　n. 轨道，足迹，踪迹，小道 |
| n. 宗教，宗教信仰 | v. 领导或参加运动　n. 运动，活动，战役 |
| adj. 最低的，最小限度的 | v. 促进，增加　n. 推动，帮助，宣扬 |
| n. 量，数量，大量 | v. 褪色，凋谢，逐渐消失 |
| v. 保证，确保 | n. 平等，相等 |
| v. 产生，造成 | v. 应付，处理（难题或局面） |
| v. 触发，引起　n. 扳机，起因 | adj. 创造性的 |
| adj. 可靠的，可信的 | adj. 令人担忧的，使人惊恐的 |
| v. 证明，展示，论证，示威 | n. 有文化的人　adj. 受过教育的，精通文学的 |
| v. 踌躇，犹豫，不愿 | n. 观点，远景　adj. 透视的 |

# DAY 17 单词

engage [ɪn'geɪdʒ]

discipline ['dɪsəplɪn]

boast [bəʊst]

outdated [ˌaʊt'deɪtɪd]

accumulate [ə'kjuːmjəleɪt]

countless ['kaʊntləs]

giant ['dʒaɪənt]

exceed [ɪk'siːd]

annual ['ænjʊəl]

collective [kə'lektɪv]

principal ['prɪnsəpl]

suspect [sə'spekt; 'sʌspekt]

contract [kən'trækt; 'kɒntrækt]

definite ['defɪnət]

casual ['kæʒʊəl]

attach [ə'tætʃ]

perceive [pə'siːv]

symptom ['sɪmptəm]

slight [slaɪt]

implication [ˌɪmplɪ'keɪʃn]

# DAY 18 单词

enforce [ɪn'fɔːs]

approve [ə'pruːv]

translate [trænz'leɪt; træns'leɪt]

prosperity [prɒ'sperətɪ]

occur [ə'kɜː(r)]

fulfill [fʊl'fɪl]

exclude [ɪk'skluːd]

crash [kræʃ]

urgent ['ɜːdʒənt]

enroll [ɪn'rəʊl]

offend [ə'fend]

scarce [skeəs]

enhance [ɪn'hɑːns]

conditional [kən'dɪʃənl]

legitimate [lɪ'dʒɪtɪmət]

allowance [ə'laʊəns]

liberate ['lɪbəreɪt]

shocking ['ʃɒkɪŋ]

profitable ['prɒfɪtəbl]

intention [ɪn'tenʃn]

# DAY 17 释义

| | |
|---|---|
| v. 吸引，占用，(使)参加，从事 | n. 校长，资本　adj. 主要的，资本的 |
| v. 训练，训导　n. 学科，纪律，训练 | v. 怀疑，**认为**　n. 犯罪嫌疑人　adj. 可疑的 |
| v. 夸口说，以有……而自豪　n. 自夸 | |
| adj. 过时的 | v. **收缩，缩短，感染**　n. 合同，契约 |
| v. 累积，积聚 | adj. 一定的，确切的 |
| adj. 无数的 | n. 便装，临时工人　adj. 随便的，**临时的** |
| n. 巨人，大公司　adj. 巨大的 | v. 使依附，贴上，系上 |
| v. 超过，胜过 | v. 察觉，感觉，理解，认知 |
| n. 年刊，年鉴　adj. 每年的 | n. 症状，征兆 |
| adj. 集体的，共同的 | v. 轻视，忽略　adj. 轻微的，少量的 |
| | n. 含义，暗示，影响 |

# DAY 18 释义

| | |
|---|---|
| v. 实施，执行，强迫 | v. 冒犯，违反 |
| v. 批准，赞成 | adj. 缺乏的，稀有的　adv. 简直不，几乎不 |
| v. 翻译，转化，转变为 | |
| n. 繁荣，成功 | v. 提高，加强 |
| v. 发生，出现，被想到 | adj. 有条件的 |
| v. 履行，实现，满足 | adj. 合法的，正当的，合理的 |
| v. 排除，排斥 | n. 津贴，零用钱 |
| v. 碰撞，(使)坠毁　n. 坠毁，暴跌，崩溃 | v. 解放，放出 |
| | adj. 令人震惊的 |
| adj. 紧急的，急迫的 | adj. 有利可图的 |
| v. 登记，注册，使加入 | n. 意图，目的 |

# DAY 19 单词

investigate [ɪn'vestɪgeɪt]

commit [kə'mɪt]

pursue [pə'sju:]

launch [lɔ:ntʃ]

grasp [grɑ:sp]

prevailing [prɪ'veɪlɪŋ]

combine [kəm'baɪn]

advocate ['ædvəkeɪt; 'ædvəkət]

function ['fʌŋkʃn]

dramatic [drə'mætɪk]

feedback ['fi:dbæk]

clarity ['klærətɪ]

proclaim [prə'kleɪm]

nevertheless [ˌnevəðə'les]

heighten ['haɪtn]

desert [dɪ'zɜ:t; 'dezət]

conserve [kən'sɜ:v]

boom [bu:m]

joint [dʒɔɪnt]

compare [kəm'peə(r)]

# DAY 20 单词

discard [dɪ'skɑ:d; 'dɪskɑ:d]

revive [rɪ'vaɪv]

procedure [prə'si:dʒə(r)]

dispute [dɪ'spju:t; 'dɪspju:t]

restrict [rɪ'strɪkt]

reluctant [rɪ'lʌktənt]

obtain [əb'teɪn]

presence ['prezns]

embrace [ɪm'breɪs]

defeat [dɪ'fi:t]

bonus ['bəʊnəs]

monitor ['mɒnɪtə(r)]

immense [ɪ'mens]

transform [træns'fɔ:m]

decrease [dɪ'kri:s; 'di:kri:s]

multiple ['mʌltɪpl]

universal [ˌju:nɪ'vɜ:sl]

champion ['tʃæmpɪən]

destructive [dɪ'strʌktɪv]

reshape [ˌri:'ʃeɪp]

# DAY 19 释义

| | |
|---|---|
| v. 调查，研究 | n. 反馈 |
| v. 犯罪，使……承担义务，承诺 | n. 清楚，清晰 |
| v. 追求，从事，追赶 | v. 宣告，声明 |
| v. 发射，发起，发动　n. 发射，发行 | adv. 然而，不过　conj. 然而，不过 |
| v. 抓牢，握紧，**理解，领悟**　n. 抓，握，**理解** | v. 提高，加强 |
| | v. **遗弃，舍弃**　n. 沙漠，荒原 |
| adj. 流行的，占优势的 | v. 节约，节省，保存 |
| v. (使)联合，(使)结合 | v. 使兴旺　n. 繁荣 |
| v. 提倡，拥护　n. 拥护者 | n. 关节　adj. 联合的，共同的 |
| n. 功能，职责 | v. 比较，对比 |
| adj. 戏剧的，急剧的，引人注目的 | |

# DAY 20 释义

| | |
|---|---|
| v. 抛弃，放弃　n. 抛弃，被丢弃的东西或人 | n. 奖金，红利，额外津贴 |
| | v. 监控　n. 监视器，显示屏 |
| v. (使)复兴，复活，苏醒 | adj. 巨大的，广大的 |
| n. 程序，步骤 | v. 改变，转换 |
| v. 辩论，争论　n. 辩论 | v. 减少，减小　n. 减少，减小 |
| v. 限制，约束 | adj. 多重的，多样的，许多的 |
| adj. 不情愿的，勉强的 | adj. 普遍的，通用的，宇宙的 |
| v. 得到，获得 | v. **支持，拥护**　n. 冠军，拥护者 |
| n. 存在，出席 | adj. 破坏的，毁灭性的 |
| v. 拥抱，欣然接受　n. 拥抱 | v. 改造，重塑 |
| v. 击败，挫败(某人)　n. 失败；战胜 | |

# DAY 21 单词

effect [ɪ'fekt]

access ['ækses]

screen [skri:n]

massive ['mæsɪv]

accuse [ə'kju:z]

operational [ˌɒpə'reɪʃənl]

target ['tɑ:gɪt]

ease [i:z]

federal ['fedərəl]

contradict [ˌkɒntrə'dɪkt]

outweigh [ˌaʊt'weɪ]

supervise ['su:pəvaɪz; 'sju:pəvaɪz]

profound [prə'faʊnd]

illustrate ['ɪləstreɪt]

accustom [ə'kʌstəm]

extensive [ɪk'stensɪv]

permission [pə'mɪʃn]

disrupt [dɪs'rʌpt]

ethical ['eθɪkl]

collapse [kə'læps]

# DAY 22 单词

response [rɪ'spɒns]

grant [grɑ:nt]

crucial ['kru:ʃl]

principle ['prɪnsəpl]

promising ['prɒmɪsɪŋ]

numerous ['nju:mərəs]

candidate ['kændɪdət; 'kændɪdeɪt]

precious ['preʃəs]

cultivate ['kʌltɪveɪt]

address [ə'dres]

distort [dɪ'stɔ:t]

accessible [ək'sesəbl]

permanent ['pɜ:mənənt]

property ['prɒpətɪ]

modify ['mɒdɪfaɪ]

impair [ɪm'peə(r)]

cater ['keɪtə(r)]

renewable [rɪ'nju:əbl]

inevitable [ɪn'evɪtəbl]

tend [tend]

# DAY 21 释义

| | |
|---|---|
| v. **产生，达到目的** n. 影响，效果 | v. （在重量上）比……重，比……重要 |
| v. 接近，使用 n. 通道，进入，使用权 | v. 监督，管理 |
| v. **筛选，检查** n. 屏幕 | adj. 深厚的，意义深远的 |
| adj. 大量的，巨大的 | v. 阐明，举例说明 |
| v. 控告，指控 | v. 使习惯于，使适应 |
| adj. 操作的，运作的 | adj. 广泛的，大量的 |
| v. 把……作为目标，对准 n. 目标，指标 | n. 允许，许可 |
| v. 减轻，缓解 n. 容易，舒适 | v. 破坏，使瓦解，使中断 |
| adj. 联邦的 | adj. 伦理的，道德的 |
| v. 反驳，否定，与……矛盾 | v. 倒塌，崩溃 n. 崩溃，（货币）暴跌 |

# DAY 22 释义

| | |
|---|---|
| n. 响应，反应 | v. 扭曲，使失真 |
| v. 授予，允许，承认 n.（政府）拨款，授予 | adj. 易接近的，可进入的，可理解的 |
| adj. 重要的，决定性的 | adj. 永久的，永恒的 |
| n. 原理，原则 | n. 性质，性能，财产，所有权 |
| adj. 有希望的，有前途的 | v. 修改，修饰 |
| adj. 许多的，很多的 | v. 损害，削弱 |
| n. 候选人，应试者 | v. 投合，迎合，满足需要 |
| adj. 宝贵的 | adj. 可再生的，可更新的 |
| v. 培养，耕作 | adj. 必然的，不可避免的 |
| v. 演说，**设法解决** n. 地址，演讲 | v. 趋向，倾向，**照料，照顾** |

# DAY 23 单词

reveal [rɪˈviːl]

incline [ɪnˈklaɪn; ˈɪnklaɪn]

intellectual [ˌɪntəˈlektʃʊəl]

obligation [ˌɒblɪˈgeɪʃn]

attain [əˈteɪn]

subject [səbˈdʒekt; ˈsʌbdʒɪkt; ˈsʌbdʒekt]

interfere [ˌɪntəˈfɪə(r)]

dismiss [dɪsˈmɪs]

content [kənˈtent; ˈkɒntent; kənˈtent]

specific [spəˈsɪfɪk]

delete [dɪˈliːt]

foresight [ˈfɔːsaɪt]

internal [ɪnˈtɜːnl]

review [rɪˈvjuː]

degrade [dɪˈgreɪd]

scheme [skiːm]

register [ˈredʒɪstə(r)]

exception [ɪkˈsepʃn]

pursuit [pəˈsjuːt]

orient [ˈɔːrient]

# DAY 24 单词

witness [ˈwɪtnəs]

priority [praɪˈɒrətɪ]

assumption [əˈsʌmpʃn]

endure [ɪnˈdjʊə(r)]

arrest [əˈrest]

stimulate [ˈstɪmjʊleɪt]

navigate [ˈnævɪgeɪt]

rigid [ˈrɪdʒɪd]

licence [ˈlaɪsns]

provision [prəˈvɪʒn]

precise [prɪˈsaɪs]

bound [baʊnd]

anticipate [ænˈtɪsɪpeɪt]

assess [əˈses]

distract [dɪˈstrækt]

confine [kənˈfaɪn]

recession [rɪˈseʃn]

executive [ɪgˈzekjətɪv]

routine [ruːˈtiːn]

proportion [prəˈpɔːʃn]

## DAY 23 释义

| | |
|---|---|
| v. 显示，透露，揭露　n. 揭露，暴露 | v. 删除 |
| v. 倾向于　n. 斜坡，斜面 | n. 先见，远见 |
| n. 知识分子　adj. 才智的，理智的 | adj. 内部的，体内的，国内的 |
| n. 义务，职责 | v. 回顾，检查，复审　n. 回顾，复习，评论 |
| v. 达到，实现，获得 | |
| v. (使)遭受　n. 实验对象　adj. 易遭受……的 | v. 贬低，(使)降级 |
| | v. 计划　n. 计划，组合，体制 |
| v. 干涉，妨碍，打扰 | v. 登记，注册，表达　n. 登记表，登记注册 |
| v. 解散，解雇，不予理会 | |
| v. 使满意　n. 内容，目录，满足　adj. 满意的 | n. 例外，异议 |
| | n. 追赶，追求，职业 |
| n. 特性，细节　adj. 特殊的，特定的 | v. 朝向，确定方位，使适应 |

## DAY 24 释义

| | |
|---|---|
| v. 目击，证明　n. 证人，目击者 | adj. 精确的，明确的 |
| n. 优先，优先权 | n. 界限　adj. 一定会，受约束的，有义务的 |
| n. 假定，设想 | |
| v. 忍耐，容忍，持续 | v. 预料，预期 |
| v. 逮捕，吸引　n. 逮捕，监禁 | v. 评定，估价 |
| v. 刺激，鼓舞，激励 | v. 转移，分心 |
| v. 导航，航行，驾驶 | v. 限制，禁闭　n. 范围，限制 |
| adj. 严格的，僵硬的，死板的 | n. 衰退，不景气 |
| v. 许可，特许　n. 执照，许可证，特许 | n. 主管，行政领导　adj. 有执行权的，高级的 |
| n. 规定，条款，供应品 | n. 常规，惯例　adj. 常规的，例行的 |
| | n. 比例，占比 |

# DAY 25 单词

contend [kən'tend]

relevant ['reləvənt]

initiative [ɪ'nɪʃətɪv]

exert [ɪg'zɜːt]

aggressive [ə'gresɪv]

obesity [əʊ'biːsətɪ]

surround [sə'raʊnd]

ancient ['eɪnʃənt]

inhabitant [ɪn'hæbɪtənt]

surpass [sə'pɑːs]

soften ['sɒfn]

qualify ['kwɒlɪfaɪ]

severe [sɪ'vɪə(r)]

terminate ['tɜːmɪneɪt]

lobby ['lɒbɪ]

compulsory [kəm'pʌlsərɪ]

perception [pə'sepʃn]

valid ['vælɪd]

intuitive [ɪn'tjuːɪtɪv]

evaluate [ɪ'væljʊeɪt]

# DAY 26 单词

deceptive [dɪ'septɪv]

logical ['lɒdʒɪkl]

refute [rɪ'fjuːt]

conservative [kən'sɜːvətɪv]

evolve [ɪ'vɒlv]

chronic ['krɒnɪk]

delay [dɪ'leɪ]

random ['rændəm]

corporation [ˌkɔːpə'reɪʃn]

wander ['wɒndə(r)]

shift [ʃɪft]

welfare ['welfeə(r)]

exercise ['eksəsaɪz]

democratic [ˌdemə'krætɪk]

consistent [kən'sɪstənt]

vanish ['vænɪʃ]

fuel ['fjuːəl]

alternative [ɔːl'tɜːnətɪv]

fashion ['fæʃn]

tension ['tenʃn]

## DAY 25 释义

| | |
|---|---|
| v. 竞争，奋斗，争论，主张 | v. 使温和，使缓和，减轻 |
| adj. 相关的，切题的，中肯的 | v. 限定，使具有资格，取得资格 |
| n. 倡议，主动权，首创精神 | adj. 严峻的，严厉的，剧烈的 |
| v. 运用，发挥，施以影响 | v.（使）终止，（使）结束，解雇 |
| adj. 侵略性的，好斗的，有进取心的 | v. 游说  n. 大厅，休息室，游说团体 |
| n. 肥胖 | adj. 义务的，必修的，被强制的 |
| v. 围绕，包围 | n. 认识能力，知觉，感觉，洞察力 |
| n. 古代人  adj. 古代的，古老的，过时的 | adj. 有效的，有根据的，合法的，正当的 |
| n. 居民，居住者 | adj. 直觉的 |
| v. 超越，胜过，优于 | v. 评价，估价 |

## DAY 26 释义

| | |
|---|---|
| adj. 欺诈的，迷惑的，虚伪的 | v. 转移，改变  n. 转移，改变，转变 |
| adj. 合逻辑的，合理的 | n. 福利，幸福  adj. 福利的 |
| v. 反驳，驳斥 | v. 锻炼，练习，使用，运用  n. 练习，运用 |
| n. 保守派，守旧者  adj. 保守的 | adj. 民主的，大众的 |
| v. 发展，进化 | adj. 始终如一的，一致的，坚持的 |
| adj. 慢性的，长期的 | v. 消失，使消失 |
| v. 延期，（使）耽搁，推迟  n. 延期，延时 | v. 提供燃料，刺激，煽动  n. 燃料，刺激因素 |
| n. 随意  adj. 随机的，任意的 | n. 供替代的选择  adj. 供选择的，交替的 |
| n. 公司，法人（团体） | v. 塑造，制定  n. 时尚，方式 |
| v. 徘徊，漫步，迷路，离题 | v. 使紧张，使拉紧  n. 张力，拉力，紧张 |

## DAY 27 单词

| | |
|---|---|
| bias ['baɪəs] | finance ['faɪnæns; faɪ'næns; fə'næns] |
| convert [kən'vɜ:t] | susceptible [sə'septəbl] |
| gender ['dʒendə(r)] | ambitious [æm'bɪʃəs] |
| current ['kʌrənt] | spark [spɑ:k] |
| outline ['aʊtlaɪn] | vehicle ['vi:əkl] |
| dominate ['dɒmɪneɪt] | upgrade ['ʌpgreɪd] |
| remarkable [rɪ'mɑ:kəbl] | existing [ɪg'zɪstɪŋ] |
| appeal [ə'pi:l] | minimize ['mɪnɪmaɪz] |
| relatively ['relətɪvli] | diligent ['dɪlɪdʒənt] |
| status ['steɪtəs] | lessen ['lesn] |

## DAY 28 单词

| | |
|---|---|
| excessive [ɪk'sesɪv] | subscribe [səb'skraɪb] |
| coordinate [kəʊ'ɔ:dɪneɪt] | thrive [θraɪv] |
| shrink [ʃrɪŋk] | diminish [dɪ'mɪnɪʃ] |
| ecology [ɪ'kɒlədʒɪ] | immune [ɪ'mju:n] |
| integrate ['ɪntɪgreɪt] | assume [ə'sju:m] |
| abstract [æb'strækt; 'æbstrækt] | widespread ['waɪdspred] |
| device [dɪ'vaɪs] | costly ['kɒstlɪ] |
| harbor ['hɑ:bə] | initially [ɪ'nɪʃəlɪ] |
| popularize ['pɒpjələraɪz] | rewarding [rɪ'wɔ:dɪŋ] |
| virtue ['vɜ:tʃu:] | charity ['tʃærətɪ] |

# DAY 27 释义

| | |
|---|---|
| *v.* 使存偏见 *n.* 偏见，偏爱 | *v.* 提供资金 *n.* 财政，金融 |
| *v.* (使)转变，转换 | *adj.* 易受影响的，易感动的 |
| *n.* 性别 | *adj.* 野心勃勃的，有雄心的 |
| *n.* 水流，电流，趋势 *adj.* 现在的，流通的 | *v.* 点燃，导致 *n.* 火花 |
| *v.* 概述，略述 *n.* 轮廓，大纲，概要 | *n.* 车辆，传播媒介 |
| *v.* 控制，支配，占优势 | *v.* 升级，改善 *n.* 升级 |
| *adj.* 卓越的，非凡的，值得注意的 | *adj.* 存在的，现行的 |
| *v.* 呼吁，上诉，吸引 *n.* 呼吁，上诉，吸引力 | *v.* 使减到最少，最小化 |
| *adv.* 相当地，相对地 | *adj.* 勤勉的，用功的 |
| *n.* 地位，状态，重要身份 | *v.* 减少，减轻，变小 |

# DAY 28 释义

| | |
|---|---|
| *adj.* 过多的，极度的 | *v.* 订阅，赞成，签署 |
| *v.* 调节，配合，协调 | *v.* 繁荣，兴旺 |
| *v.* (使)缩小，(使)收缩 | *v.* (使)减少，(使)变小 |
| *n.* 生态学 | *adj.* 免疫的，免于……的 |
| *v.* 使……完整，使……成整体 *adj.* 整合的 | *v.* 设想，承担，采取 |
| *v.* 摘要，提取 *n.* 摘要 *adj.* 理论的，抽象的 | *adj.* 普遍的，广泛的 |
| *n.* 装置，策略，设备 | *adj.* 昂贵的，代价高的 |
| *v.* 庇护，窝藏，怀有 *n.* 港，海港，避难所 | *adv.* 最初，首先 |
| *v.* 普及 | *adj.* 有益的，值得的 |
| *n.* 美德，优点 | *n.* 慈善，施舍，慈善团体 |

## DAY 29 单词

| | |
|---|---|
| wear [weə(r)] | respect [rɪ'spekt] |
| slim [slɪm] | traffic ['træfɪk] |
| isolate ['aɪsəleɪt] | skeptical ['skeptɪkl] |
| mature [mə'tʃʊə(r); mə'tjʊə(r)] | prone [prəʊn] |
| sacrifice ['sækrɪfaɪs] | eliminate [ɪ'lɪmɪneɪt] |
| prospect [prə'spekt; 'prɒspekt] | rival ['raɪvl] |
| underestimate [ˌʌndər'estɪmeɪt; ˌʌndər'estɪmət] | feature ['fi:tʃə(r)] |
| agency ['eɪdʒənsɪ] | modest ['mɒdɪst] |
| highlight ['haɪlaɪt] | imitate ['ɪmɪteɪt] |
| subsidy ['sʌbsədɪ] | adventure [əd'ventʃə(r)] |

## DAY 30 单词

| | |
|---|---|
| infinite ['ɪnfɪnət] | participate [pɑ'tɪsɪpeɪt] |
| strive [straɪv] | alter ['ɔ:ltə(r)] |
| owe [əʊ] | guideline ['gaɪdlaɪn] |
| ground [graʊnd] | elite [eɪ'li:t; ɪ'li:t] |
| collaborate [kə'læbəreɪt] | inherent [ɪn'herənt; ɪn'hɪərənt] |
| extinct [ɪk'stɪŋkt] | substitute ['sʌbstɪtju:t] |
| rational ['ræʃnəl] | lengthy ['leŋθɪ] |
| strategy ['strætədʒɪ] | absence ['æbsəns] |
| inferior [ɪn'fɪərɪə(r)] | fruitful ['fru:tfl] |
| correspond [ˌkɒrə'spɒnd] | disorder [dɪs'ɔ:də(r)] |

# DAY 29 释义

| | |
|---|---|
| v. 穿，戴，**耗损**，**耐用** | v. 尊敬，尊重　n. 尊敬，尊重，**方面** |
| v. **缩减**　adj. 苗条的，微小的 | v. 用……作交换　n. 交通，贸易，[**通信**] 通信量 |
| v. (使) 隔离，孤立 | adj. 怀疑的 |
| v. (使) 成熟　adj. 成熟的 | adj. 有……倾向的，易于……的 |
| v. 牺牲，献祭　n. 牺牲，祭品，供奉 | v. 消除，排除 |
| v. 勘探　n. 前途，预期，景色 | v. 与……竞争，比得上　n. 竞争对手 |
| v. 低估，看轻　n. 低估 | v. 特写，以……为特色，由……主演 |
| n. 代理，中介，地区政府 | n. 特色 |
| v. 突出，强调，使显著　n. 最精彩的部分 | adj. 谦虚的，谦逊的，适度的 |
| n. 补贴，津贴 | v. 模仿，仿效 |
| | v. 冒险　n. 冒险，投机活动 |

# DAY 30 释义

| | |
|---|---|
| adj. 无限的，无穷的 | v. 参与，参加，分享 |
| v. 努力，奋斗，抗争 | v. 改变，更改 |
| v. 感激，应给予，把……归功于 | n. 指导方针 |
| v. 打基础　n. 地面，**根据**，**依据** | n. 精英，精华 |
| v. 合作 | adj. 固有的，内在的，遗传的 |
| adj. 灭绝的，绝种的 | v. 替代　n. 代用品，代替者 |
| adj. 合理的，理性的 | adj. 漫长的，冗长的 |
| n. 战略，策略 | n. 没有，缺乏，缺席 |
| adj. 差的，自卑的，下级的 | adj. 富有成效的，多产的 |
| v. 符合，一致，相应，通信 | v. 使失调　n. 混乱 |

# 第二部分

## 80+必备学术词汇

### DAY 31 单词

infrastructure ['ɪnfrəstrʌktʃə(r)]

successive [sək'sesɪv]

plausible ['plɔ:zəbl]

counterpart ['kaʊntəpɑ:t]

dilemma [dɪ'lemə; daɪ'lemə]

constraint [kən'streɪnt]

absurd [əb's3:d]

ambiguous [æm'bɪgjʊəs]

contempt [kən'tempt]

integrity [ɪn'tegrətɪ]

assemble [ə'sembl]

predominant [prɪ'dɒmɪnənt]

evaporate [ɪ'væpəreɪt]

deprive [dɪ'praɪv]

unparalleled [ʌn'pærəleld]

impartial [ɪm'pɑ:ʃl]

opponent [ə'pəʊnənt]

squeeze [skwi:z]

exaggerate [ɪg'zædʒəreɪt]

intricate ['ɪntrɪkət]

### DAY 32 单词

overestimate [əʊvər'ɛstɪmeɪt; əʊvər'estɪmət]

conceive [kən'si:v]

supplement [sʌplɪ'ment; 'sʌplɪmənt]

acclaim [ə'kleɪm]

insidious [ɪn'sɪdɪəs]

vocational [vəʊ'keɪʃənl]

intervention [ˌɪntə'venʃn]

paradox ['pærədɒks]

prompt [prɒmpt]

astonishing [ə'stɒnɪʃɪŋ]

explicit [ɪk'splɪsɪt]

trivial ['trɪvɪəl]

frugal ['fru:gl]

stagnation [stæg'neɪʃn]

reckless ['rekləs]

resent [rɪ'zent]

discern [dɪ's3:n]

attribute [ə'trɪbju:t; 'ætrɪbju:t]

margin ['mɑ:dʒɪn]

curb [k3:b]

# DAY 31 释义

| | |
|---|---|
| *n.* 基础设施，公共建设 | *v.* 集合，聚集，装配 |
| *adj.* 连续的，继承的，依次的 | *adj.* 主要的，卓越的，支配的 |
| *adj.* 有道理的，可信的 | *v.* (使)蒸发，(使)消失 |
| *n.* 相对应的人或物 | *v.* 使丧失，剥夺 |
| *n.* 困境，进退两难 | *adj.* 无比的，无双的 |
| *n.* 约束，强制，限制 | *adj.* 公平的，公正的 |
| *n.* 荒诞的事物　*adj.* 荒谬的，可笑的 | *n.* 对手，反对者 |
| *adj.* 模糊不清的，不明确的 | *v.* 挤，紧握，勒索，压榨　*n.* 挤压 |
| *n.* 轻视，蔑视 | *v.* 夸大，夸张 |
| *n.* 完整，正直，诚实，廉正 | *adj.* 复杂的，错综的 |

# DAY 32 释义

| | |
|---|---|
| *v.* 高估　*n.* 高估 | *adj.* 明确的，直率的，详述的 |
| *v.* 怀孕，构思，以为 | *adj.* 不重要的，琐碎的 |
| *v.* 增补，补充　*n.* 增补(物)，增刊 | *adj.* 节俭的，朴素的 |
| *v.* 称赞，喝彩　*n.* 称赞，欢呼，喝彩 | *n.* 停滞 |
| *adj.* 阴险的，隐伏的，狡猾的 | *adj.* 鲁莽的，不顾后果的 |
| *adj.* 职业的，行业的 | *v.* 怨恨，愤恨 |
| *n.* 介入，调停，妨碍 | *v.* 识别，辨别 |
| *n.* 悖论，反论 | *v.* 归属，把……归于　*n.* 属性，特质 |
| *v.* 鼓励，促进，激起　*adj.* 敏捷的，迅速的 | *n.* 边缘，利润 |
| *adj.* 惊人的，令人惊讶的 | *v.* 控制，勒住　*n.* 抑制 |

# DAY 33 单词

vulnerable ['vʌlnərəbl]

impose [ɪm'pəʊz]

accountable [ə'kaʊntəbl]

inconceivable [ˌɪnkən'siːvəbl]

hypothesis [haɪ'pɒθəsɪs]

overwhelm [ˌəʊvə'welm]

conceal [kən'siːl]

resist [rɪ'zɪst]

aggravate ['ægrəveɪt]

indispensable [ˌɪndɪ'spensəbl]

eligible ['elɪdʒəbl]

counterbalance [ˌkaʊntə'bæləns; 'kaʊntəˌbæl(ə)ns]

speculate ['spekjʊleɪt]

acquisition [ˌækwɪ'zɪʃn]

resemble [rɪ'zembl]

privilege ['prɪvəlɪdʒ]

quota ['kwəʊtə]

discriminate [dɪ'skrɪmɪneɪt]

mandate ['mændeɪt]

controversial [ˌkɒntrə'vɜːʃl]

# DAY 34 单词

contemplate ['kɒntəmpleɪt]

transient ['trænzɪənt]

consensus [kən'sensəs]

incentive [ɪn'sentɪv]

identical [aɪ'dentɪkl]

penalty ['penəltɪ]

foreshadow [fɔː'ʃædəʊ]

transparent [træns'pærənt]

overrule [ˌəʊvə'ruːl]

comply [kəm'plaɪ]

transition [træn'zɪʃn; træn'sɪʃn]

conform [kən'fɔːm]

overturn [ˌəʊvə'tɜːn; 'əʊvətɜːn]

offset ['ɒfset]

disproportionately [ˌdɪsprə'pɔːʃənətlɪ]

underline [ˌʌndə'laɪn]

looming ['luːmɪŋ]

foster ['fɒstə(r)]

verify ['verɪfaɪ]

monopoly [mə'nɒpəlɪ]

# DAY 33 释义

| | |
|---|---|
| adj. 易受攻击的，易受伤害的 | adj. 合格的，符合条件的 |
| v. 强加，征税，利用 | v. 使平衡，抵消　n. 平衡力 |
| adj. 有责任的，可解释的 | v. 推测，投机，思索 |
| adj. 不可思议的，不能想象的 | n. 获得物，获得，收购 |
| n. 假设 | v. 类似，像 |
| v. 淹没，压倒，压垮 | v. 给予……特权　n. 特权，优待 |
| v. 隐藏，隐瞒 | n. 定额，限额，配额 |
| v. 抵抗，抗拒 | v. 歧视，区别，辨别 |
| v. 加重，使恶化 | n. 授权，命令，指令　v. 授权，托管 |
| adj. 不可缺少的 | adj. 有争议的 |

# DAY 34 释义

| | |
|---|---|
| v. 沉思，冥想，深思熟虑 | n. 过渡，转变 |
| adj. 短暂的，路过的 | v.（使）遵守，（使）一致 |
| n. 一致，合意 | v. 推翻，倾覆，破坏　n. 倾覆，周转 |
| n. 动机，刺激 | v. 抵消，弥补　n. 抵消，补偿 |
| adj. 同一的，完全相同的 | adv. 不成比例地 |
| n. 罚款，罚金，处罚 | v. 强调，在……下面画线 |
| v. 预示，成为……的前兆　n. 预兆 | adj. 逼近的，若隐若现的 |
| adj. 透明的，显然的，坦率的，易懂的 | v. 促进，抚育　adj. 寄养的 |
| v. 否决 | v. 核实，查证 |
| v. 遵守，顺从，遵从 | n. 垄断 |

# DAY 35 单词

| | |
|---|---|
| **counteract** [ˌkaʊntərˈækt] | **flawed** [flɔːd] |
| **scrutinize** [ˈskruːtənaɪz] | **sponsor** [ˈspɒnsə(r)] |
| **aggregate** [ˈægrɪgeɪt; ˈægrɪgət] | **unanimous** [juˈnænɪməs] |
| **liability** [ˌlaɪəˈbɪlətɪ] | **sarcastic** [sɑːˈkæstɪk] |
| **status quo** [ˌsteɪtəs ˈkwəʊ] | **reinforce** [ˌriːɪnˈfɔːs] |
| **undermine** [ˌʌndəˈmaɪn] | **conviction** [kənˈvɪkʃn] |
| **fatal** [ˈfeɪtl] | **uplifting** [ˌʌpˈlɪftɪŋ] |
| **worship** [ˈwɜːʃɪp] | **intrigue** [ɪnˈtriːg] |
| **humiliate** [hjuːˈmɪlieɪt] | **sanction** [ˈsæŋkʃn] |
| **compromise** [ˈkɒmprəmaɪz] | **concrete** [ˈkɒŋkriːt] |

# DAY 36 单词

| | |
|---|---|
| **endorse** [ɪnˈdɔːs] | **embody** [ɪmˈbɒdɪ] |
| **sentiment** [ˈsentɪmənt] | **inherit** [ɪnˈherɪt] |
| **overshadow** [ˌəʊvəˈʃædəʊ] | **onerous** [ˈəʊnərəs] |
| **dwarf** [dwɔːf] | **implement** [ˈɪmplɪment; ˈɪmplɪmənt] |
| **obsess** [əbˈses] | **erase** [ɪˈreɪz] |
| **blunder** [ˈblʌndə(r)] | **dearth** [dɜːθ] |
| **facilitate** [fəˈsɪlɪteɪt] | **indulgent** [ɪnˈdʌldʒənt] |
| **augment** [ɔːgˈment; ˈɔːgment] | **zealous** [ˈzeləs] |
| **adhere** [ədˈhɪə(r)] | **hostile** [ˈhɒstaɪl] |
| **bizarre** [bɪˈzɑː(r)] | **cement** [sɪˈment] |

# DAY 35 释义

| | |
|---|---|
| v. 抵消，中和 | adj. 有缺陷的，有瑕疵的 |
| v. 细阅，详细检查 | v. 赞助，发起 n. 赞助者，主办者 |
| v. 集合，聚集 n. 合计 adj. 集合的 | adj. 全体一致的，意见一致的 |
| n. 责任，债务，倾向 | adj. 挖苦的，尖刻的 |
| n. 现状 | v. 加强，强化 n. 加强 |
| v. 破坏，渐渐破坏 | n. 定罪，确信，证明有罪 |
| adj. 致命的，重大的 | adj. 令人振奋的，使人开心的 |
| v. 崇拜，尊敬 n. 崇拜，礼拜 | v. 用诡计取得，激起……的兴趣 n. 阴谋，诡计 |
| v. 羞辱，使……丢脸 | v. 制裁，批准，鼓励 n. 制裁，认可 |
| v. 妥协，使陷入危险 n. 妥协，和解 | v. 凝固 n. 具体物 adj. 混凝土的，实在的 |

# DAY 36 释义

| | |
|---|---|
| v. 认可，签署，赞同 | v. 体现，使具体化 |
| n. 感情，情绪，观点 | v. 继承 |
| v. 使失色，使蒙上阴影 | adj. 繁重的，负有义务的 |
| v. 使显得矮小 n. 侏儒 adj. 矮小的 | v. 实施，实现 n. 工具，器具 |
| v. 使痴迷，使迷恋 | v. 抹去，擦除 |
| v. 犯大错 n. 大错 | n. 缺乏 |
| v. 促进，帮助，使容易 | adj. 放纵的，宽容的 |
| v. 增加，增大 n. 增加，增大 | adj. 热心的，热情的 |
| v. 坚持，依附，粘着，追随 | adj. 敌对的，怀敌意的 |
| adj. 奇异的 | v. 粘牢，巩固，确定 n. 水泥，纽带 |

# DAY 37 单词

| | |
|---|---|
| heritage ['herɪtɪdʒ] | cumbersome ['kʌmbəsəm] |
| scatter ['skætə(r)] | detrimental [ˌdetrɪ'mentl] |
| rigorous ['rɪgərəs] | disposable [dɪ'spəʊzəbl] |
| demise [dɪ'maɪz] | retrospect ['retrəspekt] |
| impressionable [ɪm'preʃənəbl] | intimidate [ɪn'tɪmɪdeɪt] |
| steady ['stedɪ] | gear [ɡɪə(r)] |
| compliment ['kɒmplɪment; 'kɒmplɪmənt] | distress [dɪ'stres] |
| genuine ['dʒenjʊɪn] | oppressive [ə'presɪv] |
| confront [kən'frʌnt] | benefactor ['benɪfæktə(r)] |
| bureaucratic [ˌbjʊərə'krætɪk] | drastic ['dræstɪk; 'drɑːstɪk] |

# DAY 38 单词

| | |
|---|---|
| ironic [aɪ'rɒnɪk] | alleviate [ə'liːvɪeɪt] |
| suppress [sə'pres] | permeate ['pɜːmɪeɪt] |
| nonsense ['nɒnsns] | mighty ['maɪtɪ] |
| incorporate [ɪn'kɔːpəreɪt; ɪn'kɔːpərət] | impulsive [ɪm'pʌlsɪv] |
| grieve [griːv] | infringe [ɪn'frɪndʒ] |
| extravagant [ɪk'strævəɡənt] | retreat [rɪ'triːt] |
| deliberate [dɪ'lɪbəreɪt; dɪ'lɪbərət] | hinder ['hɪndə(r)] |
| fragile ['frædʒaɪl] | compel [kəm'pel] |
| obscure [əb'skjʊə(r)] | thorny ['θɔːnɪ] |
| comprise [kəm'praɪz] | impoverish [ɪm'pɒvərɪʃ] |

# DAY 37 释义

| | |
|---|---|
| *n.* 遗产，传统，继承权 | *adj.* 笨重的，难处理的 |
| *v.* 撒播，散开，散布 | *adj.* 不利的，有害的 |
| *adj.* 严格的，严厉的，严密的 | *adj.* 一次性的，可自由支配的 |
| *v.* 遗赠　*n.* 死亡，终止，转让 | *v.* 回顾，追溯　*n.* 回顾，追溯 |
| *adj.* 敏感的，易受影响的 | *v.* 恐吓，威胁 |
| *v.* 稳固，使坚定　*adj.* 稳定的，沉着的 | *v.* (使)适合　*n.* 齿轮，装置 |
| *v.* 恭维，称赞　*n.* 恭维，称赞 | *v.* 使悲痛，使贫困　*n.* 危难，不幸 |
| *adj.* 真实的，真正的 | *adj.* 压迫的，沉重的，压制性的 |
| *v.* 面对，遭遇 | *n.* 恩人，捐助者 |
| *adj.* 官僚的，官僚政治的 | *adj.* 激烈的，猛烈的 |

# DAY 38 释义

| | |
|---|---|
| *adj.* 讽刺的 | *v.* 减轻，缓和 |
| *v.* 抑制，镇压 | *v.* 渗透，弥漫 |
| *n.* 胡说，废话 | *adj.* 有力的，强有力的 |
| *v.* 包含，吸收，合并　*adj.* 一体化的 | *adj.* 冲动的，受感情驱使的 |
| *v.* (使)悲伤，(使)苦恼 | *v.* 侵犯，违反，破坏 |
| *adj.* 奢侈的，浪费的 | *v.* 撤退　*n.* 撤退 |
| *v.* 仔细考虑，商议　*adj.* 故意的，深思熟虑的 | *v.* 阻碍，打扰 |
| *adj.* 易碎的 | *v.* 强迫，迫使 |
| *v.* (使)模糊，掩盖　*adj.* 昏暗的，晦涩的 | *adj.* 多刺的，棘手的 |
| *v.* 包含，由……组成 | *v.* 使贫穷，使枯竭 |

# DAY 39 单词

backfire [ˌbæk'faɪə(r)]

fabricate ['fæbrɪkeɪt]

reckon ['rekən]

comprehensive [ˌkɒmprɪ'hensɪv]

assimilate [ə'sɪməleɪt]

transfer [træns'fɜː(r); 'trænsfɜː(r)]

induce [ɪn'djuːs]

yield [jiːld]

instinctive [ɪn'stɪŋktɪv]

aftermath ['ɑːftəmæθ; 'ɑːftəmɑːθ]

asset ['æset]

elevate ['elɪveɪt]

pessimistic [ˌpesɪ'mɪstɪk]

elaborate [ɪ'læbəreɪt; ɪ'læbərət]

prudent ['pruːdnt]

deteriorate [dɪ'tɪərɪəreɪt]

intimate ['ɪntɪmət]

setback ['setbæk]

fluctuate ['flʌktʃueɪt]

illusory [ɪ'luːsərɪ]

# DAY 40 单词

devastate ['devəsteɪt]

default [dɪ'fɔːlt; 'diːfɔːlt]

resistant [rɪ'zɪstənt]

transmit [trænz'mɪt; træns'mɪt]

renaissance [rɪ'neɪsns]

precede [prɪ'siːd]

assert [ə'sɜːt]

invalidate [ɪn'vælɪdeɪt]

exclusive [ɪk'skluːsɪv]

eradicate [ɪ'rædɪkeɪt]

flourish ['flʌrɪʃ]

radical ['rædɪkl]

gloom [gluːm]

peculiar [pɪ'kjuːlɪə(r)]

hierarchical [ˌhaɪə'rɑːkɪkl]

refrain [rɪ'freɪn]

possession [pə'zeʃn]

context ['kɒntekst]

cap [kæp]

substantial [səb'stænʃl]

# DAY 39 释义

| | |
|---|---|
| v. 产生事与愿违的后果 | n. 资产，优点 |
| v. 制造，伪造 | v. 提升，举起，振奋情绪 |
| v. 测算，估计，认为 | adj. 悲观的，厌世的 |
| adj. 综合的，广泛的，有理解力的 | v. 详细阐述　adj. 精心制作的，详尽的 |
| v. 吸收，(使)同化 | adj. 谨慎的，精明的 |
| v. 转让，移交，调动　n. 转移，调动 | v. 恶化，变坏 |
| v. 诱导，引起，引诱 | n. 知己　adj. 亲密的，私人的 |
| v. 产出，屈服，放弃　n. 产量，利润 | n. 挫折，退步 |
| adj. 本能的，直觉的，天生的 | v. (使)波动 |
| n. 后果，余波 | adj. 错觉的，幻影的 |

# DAY 40 释义

| | |
|---|---|
| v. 毁灭，毁坏 | v. 繁荣，茂盛　n. 华丽辞藻 |
| v. 不履行，默认　n. 违约，拖欠，**系统默认值** | adj. 激进的，根本的，彻底的 |
| adj. 抵抗的，反抗的 | n. 昏暗，阴暗 |
| v. 传输，传播，发射 | adj. 特殊的，独特的，奇怪的 |
| n. (艺术)新生，复活 | adj. 分层的，等级体系的 |
| v. 领先，在……之前，优于 | v. 节制，克制，避免 |
| v. 维护，断言，主张 | n. 拥有，财产，领地 |
| v. 使无效，使无价值 | n. 环境，上下文 |
| adj. 独有的，排外的　n. 独家新闻 | v. 限定金额　n. 盖，帽子，**最高限额** |
| v. 根除，消灭 | adj. 大量的，实质的 |

# DAY 41 单词

| | |
|---|---|
| forecast ['fɔːkɑːst] | accidental [ˌæksɪ'dentl] |
| assign [ə'saɪn] | originate [ə'rɪdʒɪneɪt] |
| determine [dɪ't3ːmɪn] | derive [dɪ'raɪv] |
| count [kaʊnt] | inquire [ɪn'kwaɪə(r)] |
| instance ['ɪnstəns] | bankrupt ['bæŋkrʌpt] |
| uncover [ʌn'kʌvə(r)] | extend [ɪk'stend] |
| instrument ['ɪnstrəmənt] | superficial [ˌsuːpə'fɪʃl] |
| material [mə'tɪərɪəl] | expenditure [ɪk'spendɪtʃə(r)] |
| poisonous ['pɔɪzənəs] | appoint [ə'pɔɪnt] |
| dispose [dɪ'spəʊz] | nutrition [njuː'trɪʃn] |

# DAY 42 单词

| | |
|---|---|
| ordinary ['ɔːrdənerɪ] | familiar [fə'mɪlɪə(r)] |
| financial [faɪ'nænʃl] | advance [əd'vɑːns] |
| privacy ['prɪvəsɪ] | cooperate [kəʊ'ɒpəreɪt] |
| mindful ['maɪndfl] | reputation [ˌrepjʊ'teɪʃn] |
| regulate ['regjʊleɪt] | conclusive [kən'kluːsɪv] |
| resourceful [rɪ'sɔːsfl] | characteristic [ˌkærəktə'rɪstɪk] |
| detailed ['dɪteɪld] | worthwhile ['w3ːθwaɪl] |
| creature ['kriːtʃə(r)] | complain [kəm'pleɪn] |
| damage ['dæmɪdʒ] | innovation [ˌɪnə'veɪʃn] |
| retain [rɪ'teɪn] | tempt [tempt] |

# DAY 41 释义

| | |
|---|---|
| v. 预测，预报　n. 预测，预报 | adj. 偶然的，意外的 |
| v. 分配，指派 | v. 起源，产生 |
| v. 决定，确定，下定决心 | v. 获得，取得，起源于，来自 |
| v. 计数，重要，看作　n. 计算，总数 | v. 询问，调查 |
| n. 实例，例子 | v. 使破产　adj. 破产的，倒闭的 |
| v. 发现，揭露 | v. 延伸，扩大，延长，持续 |
| n. 仪器，工具，乐器 | adj. 表面的，肤浅的 |
| n. 材料，原料，素材　adj. 物质的，重要的 | n. 支出，花费 |
| adj. 有毒的 | v. 任命，指派，约定，安排 |
| v. 处理，处置，安排 | n. 营养 |

# DAY 42 释义

| | |
|---|---|
| adj. 普通的，平凡的 | adj. 熟悉的，常见的 |
| adj. 金融的，财务的 | v. 前进，推动　n. 前进，预付款　adj. 预先的 |
| n. 隐私 | |
| adj. 留心的，注意的 | v. 合作，协作 |
| v. 控制，管理，调节，调整 | n. 名声，名誉 |
| adj. 足智多谋的，机智的 | adj. 决定性的，确凿的 |
| adj. 详细的，细致的 | n. 特征，特点　adj. 特有的，独特的 |
| n. 生物，动物 | adj. 值得的，有价值的 |
| v. 损坏，损害　n. 损坏，损失，损害赔偿金 | v. 抱怨，投诉 |
| | n. 创新，革新 |
| v. 保留，保持 | v. 诱惑，引诱 |

# DAY 43 单词

weigh [weɪ]

overcome [ˌəʊvəˈkʌm]

schedule [ˈʃedjuːl]

devise [dɪˈvaɪz]

advisable [ədˈvaɪzəbl]

structure [ˈstrʌktʃə(r)]

persuasive [pəˈsweɪsɪv]

landscape [ˈlændskeɪp]

passionate [ˈpæʃnət]

coincidence [kəʊˈɪnsɪdəns]

switch [swɪtʃ]

enlighten [ɪnˈlaɪt(ə)n]

fortunate [ˈfɔːtʃənət]

incident [ˈɪnsɪdənt]

relief [rɪˈliːf]

competent [ˈkɒmpɪtənt]

insurance [ɪnˈʃʊərəns]

deceive [dɪˈsiːv]

shield [ʃiːld]

decorate [ˈdekəreɪt]

# DAY 44 单词

explosive [ɪkˈspləʊsɪv]

belong [bɪˈlɔːn]

element [ˈelɪmənt]

divide [dɪˈvaɪd]

literature [ˈlɪtrətʃə(r)]

contest [kənˈtest; ˈkɒntest]

strike [straɪk]

emphasis [ˈemfəsɪs]

boundary [ˈbaʊndərɪ]

feasible [ˈfiːzɪb(ə)l]

clarify [ˈklærɪfaɪ]

ingredient [ɪnˈɡriːdɪənt]

consist [kənˈsɪst]

disruptive [dɪsˈrʌptɪv]

probe [prəʊb]

thrill [θrɪl]

slack [slæk]

endeavor [ɪnˈdevə(r)]

unprecedented [ʌnˈpresɪdentɪd]

framework [ˈfreɪmwɜːk]

# DAY 43 释义

| | |
|---|---|
| v. 称重，权衡，衡量 | v. 切换，转变　n. 开关，改变 |
| v. 克服，战胜 | v. 启发，启迪 |
| v. 安排，预定　n. 计划（表） | adj. 幸运的 |
| v. 设计，想出 | n. 事件，事变 |
| adj. 明智的，合理的 | n. 宽慰，减轻，缓解 |
| v. 计划，组织　n. 结构，构造 | adj. 有能力的，胜任的 |
| adj. 有说服力的 | n. 保险 |
| n. 风景，景色 | v. 欺骗 |
| adj. 热情的，充满激情的 | v. 保护，保卫　n. 盾牌，保护 |
| n. 巧合，凑巧 | v. 装饰，装潢 |

# DAY 44 释义

| | |
|---|---|
| adj. 爆炸的，爆炸性的 | v. 澄清，阐明 |
| v. 属于 | n. 成分，原料 |
| n. 元素，要素 | v. 由……组成 |
| v. 划分，分开　n. 差异 | adj. 破坏性的，创新的 |
| n. 文学 | v. 探测，调查 |
| v. 争辩，提出异议　n. 比赛，竞赛 | v. 令人兴奋　n. 激动，兴奋 |
| n. 罢工，袭击　v. 打击，罢工，达到 | v. 懈怠，偷懒　adj. 松弛的，萧条的 |
| n. 重点，强调 | v. 努力　n. 努力 |
| n. 边界，界限 | adj. 前所未有的 |
| adj. 可行的 | n. 框架，构架 |

# DAY 45 单词

reserve [rɪˈzɜːv]

bother [ˈbɒðə(r)]

respective [rɪˈspektɪv]

precaution [prɪˈkɔːʃn]

momentum [məˈmentəm]

undertake [ˌʌndəˈteɪk]

tighten [ˈtaɪtn]

circulate [ˈsɜːkjəleɪt]

thick [θɪk]

inspect [ɪnˈspekt]

detect [dɪˈtekt]

feeble [ˈfiːbl]

eminent [ˈemɪnənt]

tentative [ˈtentətɪv]

render [ˈrendə(r)]

volatile [ˈvɒlətaɪl]

alliance [əˈlaɪəns]

mechanism [ˈmekənɪzəm]

restrain [rɪˈstreɪn]

illuminate [ɪˈluːmɪneɪt]

# DAY 46 单词

durable [ˈdjuːrəbl]

coherent [kəʊˈhɪərənt]

withstand [wɪðˈstænd]

turnover [ˈtɜːnəʊvə(r)]

sophisticated [səˈfɪstɪkeɪtɪd]

spontaneous [spɒnˈteɪnɪəs]

threshold [ˈθreʃhəʊld]

underlie [ˌʌndəˈlaɪ]

portrait [ˈpɔːtreɪt]

dynamic [daɪˈnæmɪk]

vicious [ˈvɪʃəs]

constrain [kənˈstreɪn]

setting [ˈsetɪŋ]

overcharge [ˌəʊvəˈtʃɑːdʒ]

characterize [ˈkærəktəraɪz]

encounter [ɪnˈkaʊntə(r)]

swing [swɪŋ]

boycott [ˈbɔɪkɒt]

external [ɪkˈstɜːnl]

likelihood [ˈlaɪklihʊd]

## DAY 45 释义

| | |
|---|---|
| v. 保留，预订，储备　n. 储备，存储 | v. 察觉，发现，探测 |
| v. 打扰，烦扰　n. 麻烦，不便 | adj. 虚弱的，无力的 |
| adj. 分别的，各自的 | adj. 杰出的，卓越的 |
| n. 预防措施，防备 | adj. 试探性的，暂定的 |
| n. 动力，势头 | v. 使成为，提供，给予 |
| v. 承担，从事，承诺 | adj. 易变的，不稳定的，易挥发的 |
| v. 收紧，加紧，变紧 | n. 联盟，同盟 |
| v. 循环，流通，传播 | n. 机制，机械装置，方法，途径 |
| adj. 厚的，浓密的，茂密的 | v. 抑制，约束，限制 |
| v. 检查，视察，检验 | v. 照亮，阐明，启发 |

## DAY 46 释义

| | |
|---|---|
| adj. 耐用的，持久的 | adj. 恶毒的，邪恶的 |
| adj. 连贯的，一致的 | v. 限制，约束 |
| v. 经受住，承受，抵挡 | n. 环境，场合，背景 |
| n. 周转率，成交量 | v. 要价过高，超载 |
| adj. 复杂的，老练的 | v. 是……的特征，描述，刻画 |
| adj. 自发的，自然的 | v. 遇到，遭遇 |
| n. 门槛，开端，起点，入门 | v. 摆动，改变　n. 摇摆，改变，变化 |
| v. 成为……的基础 | v. 抵制　n. 抵制行动 |
| n. 肖像，画像 | adj. 外部的，外来的 |
| adj. 动态的，有活力的 | n. 可能性，可能 |

# DAY 47 单词

| | |
|---|---|
| intensive [ɪn'tensɪv] | stereotype ['sterɪətaɪp] |
| consolidate [kən'sɒlɪdeɪt] | captive ['kæptɪv] |
| harsh [hɑːʃ] | manifest ['mænɪfest] |
| pledge [pledʒ] | deficient [dɪ'fɪʃnt] |
| strain [streɪn] | faint [feɪnt] |
| liberal ['lɪbərəl] | exemplify [ɪg'zemplɪfaɪ] |
| submit [səb'mɪt] | sensible ['sensəbl] |
| neutral ['njuːtrəl] | foundation [faʊn'deɪʃn] |
| reverse [rɪ'vɜːs] | sharpen ['ʃɑːpən] |
| parallel ['pærəlel] | defensive [dɪ'fensɪv] |

# DAY 48 单词

| | |
|---|---|
| punctual ['pʌŋktʃʊəl] | extinguish [ɪk'stɪŋgwɪʃ] |
| compassionate [kəm'pæʃənət] | offensive [ə'fensɪv] |
| ascertain [ˌæsə'teɪn] | instantaneous [ˌɪnstən'teɪnɪəs] |
| commemorate [kə'meməreɪt] | disperse [dɪ'spɜːs] |
| fracture ['fræktʃə(r)] | paralyze ['pærəlaɪz] |
| censorship ['sensəʃɪp] | insulate ['ɪnsjʊleɪt] |
| obedient [ə'biːdɪənt] | propagate [prə'pəgeɪt] |
| appetite ['æpɪtaɪt] | simultaneous [ˌsɪməl'teɪnɪəs] |
| invasive [ɪn'veɪsɪv] | dreadful ['dredfl] |
| hospitality [ˌhɒspɪ'tælətɪ] | prominent ['prɒmɪnənt] |

# DAY 47 释义

| | |
|---|---|
| *adj.* 加强的，密集的，集中的 | *n.* 刻板印象 |
| *v.* 使巩固，使加强，合并 | *n.* 俘虏　*adj.* 被俘虏的 |
| *adj.* 艰苦的，严厉的，严酷的 | *v.* 显示，表明　*adj.* 明显的 |
| *v.* 保证，承诺　*n.* 誓言，保证，承诺 | *adj.* 不足的，缺乏的 |
| *v.* 拉紧　*n.* 焦虑，紧张 | *adj.* 微弱的，虚弱的，模糊的 |
| *adj.* 自由的，开明的，文科的 | *v.* 例证，证明 |
| *v.* 提交，屈服 | *adj.* 理智的，合理的 |
| *adj.* 中立的，中性的 | *n.* 基础，基金会 |
| *v.* 扭转，改变，推翻　*adj.* 相反的 | *v.* 使锋利，增强，提高 |
| *v.* 比得上　*n.* 相似的事物　*adj.* 类似的 | *adj.* 防御的，防守的 |

# DAY 48 释义

| | |
|---|---|
| *adj.* 准时的，守时的 | *v.* 熄灭，扑灭 |
| *adj.* 有同情心的，怜悯的 | *adj.* 冒犯的，无礼的 |
| *v.* 确定，查明 | *adj.* 瞬间的，即时的 |
| *v.* 纪念，庆祝 | *v.* 分散，散布 |
| *v.* 破裂，瓦解，分裂　*n.* 破裂，骨折 | *v.* 使瘫痪，使麻痹 |
| *n.* 审查制度 | *v.* 隔离，使绝缘 |
| *adj.* 顺从的，听话的 | *v.* 散播，宣传，繁殖 |
| *n.* 食欲，胃口，欲望 | *adj.* 同时的，同步的 |
| *adj.* 侵入的，侵略性的 | *adj.* 可怕的，糟糕的 |
| *n.* 好客，热情款待 | *adj.* 显著的，突出的 |

# DAY 49 单词

| | |
|---|---|
| trumpet ['trʌmpɪt] | daunting ['dɔ:ntɪŋ] |
| imminent ['ɪmɪnənt] | miserable ['mɪzrəbl] |
| prosecute ['prɒsɪkju:t] | authentic [ɔ:'θentɪk] |
| corrupt [kə'rʌpt] | preach [pri:tʃ] |
| brilliant ['brɪlɪənt] | disintegrate [dɪs'ɪntɪgreɪt] |
| institution [ˌɪnstɪ'tju:ʃn] | proceed [prə'si:d] |
| striking ['straɪkɪŋ] | saturate ['sætʃəreɪt] |
| capture ['kæptʃə(r)] | meddle ['medl] |
| representative [ˌreprɪ'zentətɪv] | misinterpret [ˌmɪsɪn'təprɪt] |
| arbitrary ['ɑ:bɪtrərɪ] | disposition [ˌdɪspə'zɪʃn] |

# DAY 50 单词

| | |
|---|---|
| spectacular [spek'tækjələ(r)] | literally ['lɪtərəlɪ] |
| magnitude ['mægnɪtju:d] | stern [stɜ:n] |
| dubious ['dju:bɪəs] | abdicate ['æbdɪkeɪt] |
| nurture ['nɜ:tʃə(r)] | apprehension [ˌæprɪ'henʃn] |
| anonymous [ə'nɒnɪməs] | substantiate [səb'stænʃɪeɪt] |
| install [ɪn'stɔ:l] | forsake [fə'seɪk] |
| monarchy ['mɒnəkɪ] | allegiance [ə'li:dʒəns] |
| complement ['kɒmplɪment; 'kɒmplɪmənt] | lucrative ['lju:krətɪv] |
| statistical [stə'tɪstɪkl] | countermeasure ['kaʊntəmeʒə(r)] |
| stiff [stɪf] | reconcile ['rekənsaɪl] |

# DAY 49 释义

| | |
|---|---|
| *v.* 鼓吹，宣扬　*n.* 喇叭，小号 | *adj.* 令人畏惧的，吓人的 |
| *adj.* 即将发生的，逼近的 | *adj.* 悲惨的，痛苦的 |
| *v.* 起诉，控告 | *adj.* 真正的，真实的 |
| *v.* 使腐败，堕落　*adj.* 腐败的，贪污的 | *v.* 宣扬，传道，说教 |
| *adj.* 辉煌的，杰出的 | *v.* 使分解，使瓦解 |
| *n.* 机构，制度，建立 | *v.* 开始行动，开展 |
| *adj.* 引人注目的，显著的 | *v.* 使湿透，使饱和 |
| *v.* 俘获，捕获，占领，吸引，引起 | *v.* 干涉，管闲事 |
| *n.* 代表　*adj.* 有代表性的，典型的 | *v.* 误解，曲解 |
| *adj.* 任意的，武断的 | *n.* 性格，倾向，处置 |

# DAY 50 释义

| | |
|---|---|
| *adj.* 壮观的，惊人的 | *adv.* 照字面地，确实地，简直 |
| *n.* 巨大，重要性，规模，大小 | *adj.* 严厉的，坚定的 |
| *adj.* 可疑的，怀疑的 | *v.* 退位，放弃 |
| *v.* 培养，养育，促进　*n.* 养育，培育 | *n.* 担忧，恐惧 |
| *adj.* 匿名的，无名的 | *v.* 证实，证明 |
| *v.* 安装，安置，任命 | *v.* 放弃，抛弃 |
| *n.* 君主制，君主政体 | *n.* 忠诚，效忠 |
| *v.* 补充　*n.* 补充物，补足物 | *adj.* 有利可图的，赚钱的 |
| *adj.* 统计的，统计学的 | *n.* 对策，对抗措施 |
| *adj.* 硬的，僵硬的，严厉的 | *v.* 使和解，调和 |

# 第三部分

## 60+必备学术词汇配套练习

### DAY 1 练习

| | | | | |
|---|---|---|---|---|
| observe | applying | ceremony | recognized | solved |
| check | sensitive | optimistic | embarrassed | recommended |

**1** Before _____ for university I told everyone that I would study journalism, because writing was one of my favourite activities.

**2** My good performance in the job interview left me _____ about my future and about what I can do here.

**3** The classroom teacher must be _____ to a child's needs.

**4** _____ carefully if any change occurs when doing experiments in the lab.

**5** Last night, there were millions of people watching the opening _____ live on TV.

**6** I borrowed the book *Sherlock Holmes* from the library last week, which my classmates _____ to me.

**7** — What time is it?

— I have no idea. But just a minute, I will _____ it for you.

**8** The film star wears sunglasses. Therefore, he can go shopping without being _____.

**9** There are still many problems to be _____ before we are ready for a long stay on the Moon.

**10** Some patients are too _____ to consult their doctor about the problem.

| assistance | accompanied | mental | various | perform |
| tendency | devoted | convey | stressed | beneficial |

**1** If Mr. Dewey had been present, he would have offered any possible _____ to the people in need.

**2** Understanding your own needs and styles of communication is as important as learning to _____ your affection and emotions.

**3** You will never gain success unless you are fully _____ to your work.

**4** To free ourselves from the physical and _____ tensions, we each need deep thought and inner quietness.

**5** Children, when _____ by their parents, are allowed to enter the stadium.

**6** All we need is a small piece of land where we can plant _____ kinds of fruit trees throughout the growing seasons of the year.

**7** A new study shows students who write notes by hand during lectures _____ better on exams than those who use laptops.

**8** A good diet is _____ to health.

**9** China's leaders have _____ the need for increased co-operation between Third World countries.

**10** There is a growing _____ among employers to hire part-time staff.

## DAY 2 练习

| | | | | |
|---|---|---|---|---|
| account | recovered | intends | classified | exact |
| promoted | conduct | stood | promise | deserve |

**1** Shakespeare's writing is still popular today. It has really _____ the test of time.

**2** Waiting for the opportunity to be _____, Henry did his best to perform his duty.

**3** It is difficult to _____ for the fact that unemployment rate is still rising despite the economic recovery.

**4** He has just _____ from a serious illness, so he is still weak.

**5** The public lost faith in the government, since it failed to keep its _____ to lower taxes.

**6** The government _____ to use the money for the development of the tourist industry.

**7** The _____ year which Angela and her family spent together in China was 2008.

**8** The scientist decided to _____ an experiment to test the new theory.

**9** Some people may feel that their work is less valuable than others' and do not _____ recognition.

**10** The books in the library are _____ according to subject.

| contribute | generations | spiritual | object | admiration |
| exhibited | expand | accurate | techniques | talent |

**1** A child's vocabulary can _____ through reading.

**2** The Pompidou Centre in Paris is showing its respect and _____ for the famous artist.

**3** GDP does not include important factors, such as environmental quality or education outcomes, which can _____ to a person's sense of well-being.

**4** It's difficult to make _____ predictions about the effects of our behaviors on the environment.

**5** Many local people _____ to the building of the new airport due to the noise.

**6** I have a special feeling for this house, since my family have lived in it for _____.

**7** After improving material well-being, we should also enrich our _____ life.

**8** His work was _____ in the best galleries in America, Europe and Asia.

**9** She is proud that both her children have a _____ for music.

**10** The artist combines different _____ in the same painting.

# DAY 3 练习

| | | | | |
|---|---|---|---|---|
| afford | inform | refuse | despite | normal |
| prove | explore | achieve | guaranteed | convince |

**1** Starting your own business could be a way to _____ financial independence. On the other hand, it could just put you in debt.

**2** I don't believe what you said , but if you can prove it , you may be able to _____ me.

**3** Having spent nearly all our money , we couldn't _____ to stay at a hotel.

**4** It is unbelievable that Mr. Lucas leads a simple life _____ his great wealth .

**5** Please _____ us of any changes of address.

**6** It's _____ to feel tired after such a long trip.

**7** The job offer was simply too good to _____ .

**8** Basic human rights, including freedom of speech, are now _____ in our country.

**9** They hope this new evidence will _____ her innocence.

**10** As soon as we arrived on the island, we were eager to _____ it.

| essential | settle | claiming | acceptable | bargains |
| facilities | reduce | restore | anxious | practical |

**1** Although you can find _____ in the market, it's not generally a cheap place to shop.

**2** In the long run, it makes sense for you to _____ down and find a permanent job.

**3** There are plenty of graduates who are _____ to find ideal jobs in order to support themselves.

**4** Scientists are _____ a major breakthrough in the fight against cancer.

**5** Giving up smoking can _____ the risk of heart disease.

**6** Some philosophers insist that money is not _____ to happiness.

**7** Children must learn socially _____ behaviors.

**8** The measures are intended to _____ public confidence in the economy.

**9** The hotel has special _____ for disabled people.

**10** Students can gain _____ experience of the work by doing part-time jobs.

# DAY 4 练习

| | | | | |
|---|---|---|---|---|
| conflict | selected | curious | guilty | admit |
| acquired | puzzles | comment | raised | offend |

**1** I don't really like the author, but I have to _____ that his books are very exciting.

**2** She found herself in _____ with her parents over her future career.

**3** During her film career, she _____ a reputation as a strong-willed, outspoken woman.

**4** Young children are always _____ about the world where they live in.

**5** I feel _____ about not visiting my parents more often.

**6** The plans for the new development have _____ angry objection from local residents.

**7** The professor refused to make _____ on the government education policy.

**8** All hotels on the list have been carefully _____ for the excellent service they provide.

**9** What _____ me is why he has left the country without telling anyone.

**10** He apologizes for his comments which _____ the public.

| signal | definition | create | depend | struggles |
|--------|-----------|--------|--------|-----------|
| reminded | chased | adapt | compensated | origin |

**1** Passengers are _____ that no smoking is allowed on this train.

**2** There is no generally accepted _____ of happiness.

**3** The world will be different, and we will have to be prepared to _____ to the change.

**4** The speech from the new government is a _____ that major changes are on the way.

**5** Top graduates from universities are _____ by major companies.

**6** The _____ of the Dragon Boat Festival is to commemorate the soul of Qu Yuan.

**7** The young man _____ to support his poor family by doing different jobs.

**8** The government plans to _____ more jobs for young people.

**9** Her lawyers say she should be _____ for the suffering she had been caused.

**10** The chances of a full recovery will _____ on the severity of her injuries.

## DAY 5 练习

| | | | | |
|---|---|---|---|---|
| addition | adjusting | barriers | propose | concentrate |
| attracted | inspire | declined | impressive | diverse |

**1** As online courses gain popularity, the significance of traditional teaching has
_____.

**2** It is natural for freshmen to have difficulty in _____ to new campus life.

**3** In _____ to the school, the village has a clinic, which was also built with
government support.

**4** Teachers should _____ all students to think creatively.

**5** English is a language shared by several _____ cultures, each of which uses it
differently.

**6** The exhibition has _____ thousands of visitors each year.

**7** It is difficult for young children to _____ on studies for a long time.

**8** The author's latest book is one of the most _____ novels in recent years.

**9** Duties and taxes are common _____ to free trade.

**10** The engineer was the first person to _____ the construction of the bridge.

| aware | satisfied | occasion | criticized | gather |
| tough | express | forgive | contact | abandon |

**1** The way children talk about or _____ their feelings depends on their age and stage of development.

**2** He went through with his plan although all his friends advised him to _____ it.

**3** Many view these meetings as an _____ to share ideas and refresh friendship.

**4** Smokers are not _____ of the potential dangers to their own health.

**5** During the Mid-Autumn Festival, family members often _____ together to share a meal, watch the moon and enjoy moon cakes.

**6** Starting up a new company was a very _____ decision but we feel we have made the right one.

**7** In order to achieve true happiness, we need to be _____ with what we have.

**8** He burst into tears, begging her to _____ him and swearing to pay back everything he had stolen.

**9** The government has been _____ for not taking the problem seriously.

**10** Have you kept in _____ with any of your friends from college?

# DAY 6 练习

| | | | | |
|---|---|---|---|---|
| sufficient | purchase | grateful | attempts | confuse |
| exist | entertain | available | immediate | charge |

**1** Today we live in a world where GPS systems, digital maps, and other navigation apps are _____ on our smart phones.

**2** Our library should _____ more updated books to replace outdated ones.

**3** Do you think museums should _____ for admission?

**4** The effects of global warming, while not _____, are potentially disastrous.

**5** Most scientists believe that the moon's poles are where water is most likely to _____.

**6** There is _____ evidence to show that plastic bags have caused white pollution to the environment.

**7** Newspapers influence our opinion, educate us, _____ us, and keep us in touch with the world.

**8** The principal _____ to improve students' physical condition by updating existing sports facilities.

**9** I am extremely _____ to all the teachers for their help.

**10** Instead of providing an answer, his comments only served to _____ the issue further.

| exhausted | secure | apparent | frustrated | confirmed |
| expense | adopt | relieve | commercial | efficient |

**1** Smiling and laughing has actually been shown to _____ tension and stress.

**2** It is increasingly _____ that smart phones have transformed our communication patterns.

**3** Conscrvationists in Chile are concerned over the effect of _____ exploitation of forests.

**4** Recent medical studies have _____ the value of a healthier lifestyle.

**5** It is wrong to aim at sheer quantity at the _____ of quality.

**6** Some people work to _____ social recognition rather than to earn money.

**7** Three teams _____ different approaches to the problem.

**8** We should focus on finding methods of making _____ use of limited resources.

**9** Within three days, adventurers have _____ their supply of food. Therefore, they have to give up the exploration.

**10** When things go wrong, all of us naturally feel disappointed and _____.

# DAY 7 练习

| | | | | |
|---|---|---|---|---|
| approach | request | stubborn | reflect | predict |
| blindly | desperate | sympathy | ignore | return |

**1** Joe is proud and _____, never admitting he is wrong and always looking for someone else to blame.

**2** We most prefer to say yes to the _____ of someone we know and like.

**3** Last week a tennis ball hit me on the head, but I tried to _____ the pain, believing that it would go away sooner or later.

**4** No matter how carefully you plan your finances, no one can _____ when the unexpected crisis will happen.

**5** Facing up to your problems rather than running away from them is the best _____ to working things out.

**6** The aim of education is to teach young people to think for themselves and not follow others _____.

**7** While staying in the village, James unselfishly shared whatever he had with the villagers without asking for anything in _____.

**8** Store owners are getting _____ after two years of poor sales.

**9** Don't waste your _____ on the poor man — he got what he deserved.

**10** Our newspaper aims to _____ the views of the local community.

| occasionally | require | constant | associate | maintain |
| defend | delight | wisdom | imagine | flexible |

**1** To my _____, I was being chosen from hundreds of applicants to attend the opening ceremony.

**2** There is only one thing that people can't take away from you, and that is your _____.

**3** These pets _____ a lot of care and attention.

**4** He tries to _____ a healthy lifestyle, hoping it will reduce his chances of getting the disease.

**5** All soldiers are trained to _____ themselves against unexpected attacks.

**6** The relationship between wealth and happiness is a _____ topic that has been discussed by many philosophers of different times.

**7** _____ working hours allow employees to arrange their own time.

**8** It is impossible to _____ a life without smart phones.

**9** People often _____ peer pressure with bad behaviors, such as smoking and drinking.

**10** _____, we need to indulge in some undesirable behaviors, such as drinking, to release our stress.

# DAY 8 练习

| | | | | |
|---|---|---|---|---|
| handle | replace | innocent | shelter | prohibits |
| persuaded | organized | awaken | abundant | expose |

**1** The number of deaths from heart disease will be reduced greatly if people are _____ to eat more fruits and vegetables.

**2** Group activities will be _____ after class to help children develop team spirit.

**3** The new design will eventually _____ all existing models.

**4** The high cost of equipment _____ many people from taking up this sport.

**5** She thought that if she armed herself with knowledge and experience, she could _____ anything.

**6** The aim of the exhibition was to _____ an interest in and an understanding of foreign cultures.

**7** In ancient times, people define a happy life as a life with food and _____.

**8** Many companies shift their factories to developing regions to exploit their _____ supply of cheap labour.

**9** A wise mother will never _____ her children to the slightest possibility of danger.

**10** In English law, a person is presumed _____ until proved guilty.

| amazed | cautious | occupies | disturb | voluntary |
| contrary | primary | reasonable | accommodate | fantastic |

**1** I bought the car because it was not only good in quality but also _____ in price.

**2** If you get up early, try not to _____ everyone else.

**3** I am confident about Alibaba's future success but some remain _____ about possible risks, including its product quality.

**4** _____ to popular belief, many cats dislike milk.

**5** After retiring, she became involved in _____ service in the local community.

**6** I am sure that you will be absorbed in the _____ fiction movie.

**7** With a goal in mind, you will be _____ at your potential if you strive for that goal.

**8** It is clear that the _____ duty of parents is to provide protection for our children.

**9** Her career _____ all of her time, leaving her little time to accompany her children.

**10** The school was not big enough to _____ all the children.

# DAY 9 练习

| | | | | |
|---|---|---|---|---|
| interaction | distinguish | celebrate | conscious | scare |
| elegance | affect | conventional | absorb | process |

**1** The patient was fully _____ throughout the surgery and knew what was going on.

**2** Price changes may negatively _____ the living standards of the people.

**3** The furniture managed to combine practicality with _____.

**4** Plants can _____ carbon dioxide from the air and moisture from the soil.

**5** Teenagers may learn how to commit crimes through _____ with peers.

**6** Many cultures _____ birthdays and marriages with cakes that are cut and shared among the guests.

**7** This remarkable technology provides far greater clarity than _____ X-rays.

**8** It is difficult for young children to _____ reality from fantasy.

**9** Quitting smoking is a long and painful _____.

**10** While extreme sports may attract a large number of supporters, they also _____ away many people.

| exploit | impact | potential | documented | formal |
| strengthen | professional | recycle | regretful | aroused |

**1** Causes of the disease have been well _____ in this book.

**2** His revolutionary work in linguistics has _____ intense scholarly interest.

**3** The Green Movement in Germany has made that country a leader in the drive to _____ more waste materials.

**4** Taking part in some group activities is a good way to _____ friendships.

**5** It is obvious that the reform will have a marked _____ on the future of the country.

**6** The store owner is unwilling to make a _____ apology to the customer for the faulty product.

**7** The young player prepares to begin his _____ career in the sport.

**8** We are aware of the _____ problems and have taken every precaution.

**9** Apparently, he made the decision in haste. Now he is very _____.

**10** The country makes great efforts to _____ its potential oil and natural gas reserves.

# DAY 10 练习

| adequate | manufacture | oppose | established | vital |
|----------|-------------|--------|-------------|-------|
| effective | identified | residents | host | visible |

**1** A _____ of problems may delay the opening of the new bridge.

**2** Scientists have _____ chemicals produced by certain plants which have powerful cancer-fighting properties.

**3** The most _____ sign of the economic depression is the high unemployment rate.

**4** The progressive party strongly _____ reintroduction of old policies.

**5** Aspirin is a simple but highly _____ treatment to reduce pains.

**6** The school has _____ a successful relationship with the local community.

**7** Urban _____ are exposed to serious noise pollution.

**8** Complex machine tools are needed to _____ advanced engines.

**9** Without _____ information, many students choose a college almost blindly.

**10** Good financial accounts are _____ to the success of any company.

| remove | depressed | affirm | tolerate | sustain |
| display | estimate | reject | generous | stable |

**1** It is hard to _____ how many children suffer from under-nutrition in this area.

**2** New researches _____ the effectiveness of this drug to treat diabetes.

**3** Special procedures are needed to _____ impurities from the drinking water.

**4** Due to the limited budget, the government is likely to _____ the construction of a new high-speed railway.

**5** She managed to _____ everyone's interest until the end of her speech.

**6** He was always _____ in sharing his enormous knowledge.

**7** The ability to _____ physical pain varies from person to person.

**8** A _____ domestic environment is needed for the economic growth.

**9** The exhibition gives local artists an opportunity to _____ their work.

**10** The lower demand has _____ the housing market.

# DAY 11 练习

| | | | | |
|---|---|---|---|---|
| distributed | novel | exchange | complex | overlook |
| condemned | standard | desirable | announce | gradually |

**1** We could not afford to _____ the negative effect of white pollution.

**2** The government will _____ its plans to create a million new jobs.

**3** The structure of the human brain is so _____ that it is impossible to reproduce.

**4** The editor of the newspaper was _____ for lacking objectivity.

**5** Daily necessities are _____ by a special team in the disaster-affected area.

**6** Factory workers may be replaced by machines _____.

**7** Teachers always encourage students to put forward _____ ways to work out the math problem.

**8** A balanced diet will have a _____ effect on our physical condition.

**9** This website provides a good platform for users to _____ ideas and thoughts.

**10** You'd better lower your _____ if you want to find somewhere cheap to live.

| addicted | expand | respond | optional | justify |
| distinct | indicates | prejudice | founded | emerge |

**1** Their marriage was _____ on love and mutual respect.

**2** It is easy for teenagers who lack self-control to be _____ to online games.

**3** Schools in our city provide a variety of _____ courses to cater to students of different levels.

**4** A serious leakage of data can _____ the decision to spend heavy money on data security.

**5** In many countries, there is widespread _____ against workers over 45.

**6** Each of London's districts has a _____ character that marks it off from its neighbors.

**7** We intend to _____ the business by opening two more stores.

**8** A survey of retired people _____ that most are becoming independent and enjoying their life.

**9** This modest group size allows our teachers to _____ to the needs of each student.

**10** The cultural life of the country will definitely decline unless more writers and artists _____.

# DAY 12 练习

| | | | | |
|---|---|---|---|---|
| represent | regardless | withdraw | instant | fluently |
| burdensome | preserve | triumph | donate | fundamental |

**1** When workers retire, they can _____ money from the saving account.

**2** The rich man decides to _____ his collections to the local museum.

**3** _____ of the opposition from the majority of members, the new law was passed.

**4** A _____ debt can ruin an ordinary family.

**5** His books is an _____ success, receiving widespread acclaim.

**6** It often takes a while for new ideas to _____ over old ones.

**7** Effort should be made to _____ buildings of architectural or historic interest.

**8** The right to express freely is a _____ human right.

**9** Voters elected him to _____ wider interests of people, rather than narrow sectional interests.

**10** English has a large vocabulary with different usages so it's not easy for a Chinese person to speak English as _____ as a native speaker.

| neglect | academic | concept | reliable | acknowledge |
| release | interrupt | consequence | deliver | starve |

**1** In general, Japanese cars are very _____ and breakdowns are rare.

**2** The _____ of carbon dioxide into the atmosphere is the main cause of greenhouse effect.

**3** He devotes himself to his career, only to _____ his family.

**4** E-payment has changed the _____ of paper money.

**5** Countless workers will lose their jobs as a direct _____ of the automation.

**6** Many actresses try to _____ themselves in order to lose weight.

**7** It is difficult for people to _____ their own faults.

**8** Students will return to the campus in October for the start of the new _____ year.

**9** Do not ever _____ someone while they are talking or explaining something.

**10** Some newspapers even refuse to _____ papers to distant suburbs in order to reduce costs.

# DAY 13 练习

| | | | | |
|---|---|---|---|---|
| dedicate | productive | recruit | motivate | seize |
| shortage | accomplish | budget | enormous | accelerate |

**1** A _____ of funds is preventing scientists from continuing their research.

**2** There are not enough native-born workers in these countries so they must _____ workers from other countries.

**3** Cooperating with others may help us _____ our goal more easily.

**4** The holiday plan is designed to _____ employees to work more efficiently.

**5** The work was finished on time and within _____.

**6** The children are determined to _____ themselves to science after growing up.

**7** Long-term exposure to the sun can _____ the ageing process.

**8** Recent studies show that we will be more _____ at work if we take short breaks regularly.

**9** We are anxious to get a better education so that we can _____ the chance to have a brighter future.

**10** If such materials became generally available to the industry, payoffs from such a breakthrough would be _____.

| debate | analyze | complicated | rural | entitled |
|--------|---------|-------------|-------|----------|
| capacity | previous | moderate | persist | objective |

**1** The government believes that more money should be spent on improving public transport in _____ areas.

**2** The storage _____ of a battery will increase sharply with the development of technology.

**3** Under new situations, some people still _____ in handling matter according to old habits.

**4** We should develop the students' ability to _____ and solve problems.

**5** Consumers tend to _____ their spending during the economic depression.

**6** There has been a lot of _____ among scholars about the effect of online games on teenagers.

**7** This math problem is so _____ that it scares away many students.

**8** People will be _____ to their pension when they meet the job tenure and age requirements.

**9** Although the author has tried to be _____, the book inevitably mirrors his own interests and experiences.

**10** The current economic downturn is markedly different from _____ ones.

# DAY 14 练习

| | | | | |
|---|---|---|---|---|
| temporary | moral | assure | instruct | critical |
| invest | survive | considerable | contrast | violated |

**1** Only by protecting the environment can we _____ our later generation of a beautiful planet.

**2** Government agencies must _____ more funds in training and development programs.

**3** Adults have a _____ duty to take care of their elderly parents.

**4** A balance between life and work is _____ to improving people's overall well-being.

**5** The man went to prison because he _____ the law.

**6** Animals that are most suited to the environment will be those that will _____.

**7** Due to fear of an earthquake, local residents move into _____ shelters.

**8** Parents are supposed to _____ their children not only in words but in deeds.

**9** There is an obvious _____ between the cultures of East and West.

**10** The project has demanded _____ investment of time and effort.

| surface | arrange | construction | original | crisis |
| intelligent | favorable | appropriate | domestic | interpreted |

**1** Now that the problem has been identified, _____ action can be taken.

**2** She will try to _____ a convenient time and place for an interview.

**3** The company is still in _____ but it has survived the worst of the depression.

**4** To use the iPads as e-readers in place of traditional textbooks is an _____ idea.

**5** As large quantities of plastic bags have been used, the issue of white pollution begins to _____.

**6** Microwave oven is one of the most common _____ appliances.

**7** We tend to believe that all human beings are much more _____ than animals.

**8** The majority of students believe that learning English well will put them in a _____ position in the future job markets.

**9** The poem can be _____ in many different ways.

**10** Shortage of laborers slows down the _____ of this new bridge.

# DAY 15 练习

| | | | | |
|---|---|---|---|---|
| enthusiastic | atmosphere | threaten | passive | capable |
| circumstances | harmony | considerate | survey | appreciate |

**1** The machines directly _____ the livelihood of the established workers.

**2** A recent _____ shows 75% of people interviewed were in favour of the plan.

**3** Watching TV programs is a _____ process rather than an active one.

**4** Human life is regarded as part of nature, and the only way for us to survive is to live in _____ with nature.

**5** Children, on the other hand, are supposed to _____ what their parents have done for them.

**6** Graduates should be encouraged to make a suitable choice according to their personal _____.

**7** Reducing levels of carbon dioxide in the _____ is of critical importance.

**8** She is always polite and _____ towards her employees.

**9** It is generally acknowledged that human beings differ from animals in that humans are _____ of using language.

**10** He is an _____ supporter of animal rights, insisting that animal tests are cruel, inhumane and unnecessary.

| calculate | revenue | indifferent | obstacle | capital |
| reproduce | emphasizes | inflation | artificial | mutual |

**1** The _____ from tourism is the biggest single item in the country's earnings.

**2** It is illegal to _____ these worksheets without permission from the publisher.

**3** It is regrettable that people have become _____ to the suffering of others.

**4** Researchers found that too much _____ light at night can alter mood and lead to some symptoms, such as lack of energy or enthusiasm.

**5** A lack of qualifications can be a major _____ to finding an ideal job.

**6** Parents and their children should communicate with each other frequently so as to promote _____ understanding.

**7** Although the government is taking steps to limit _____, prices of goods are still rising.

**8** Biologists _____ that there are about 20,000–25,000 polar bears worldwide.

**9** His speech _____ the importance of attracting industry to the town.

**10** If you plan to set up a new business, you must have sufficient _____.

# DAY 16 练习

| | | | | |
|---|---|---|---|---|
| quantity | minimal | generate | proper | ensure |
| credible | trigger | religion | demonstrates | hesitate |

**1** It is impossible to gain _____ and reliable information from a single source.

**2** The law states that everyone has the right to practise their own _____.

**3** Too much stress may _____ serious mental illness.

**4** In order to save money, scientists carry out their work at _____ cost.

**5** We must _____ that all children have access to high quality education.

**6** Please do not _____ to contact me if you have any queries with regard to this project.

**7** The study also _____ a direct link between obesity and mortality.

**8** A well-known physician points out that hearts and bodies need _____ exercise.

**9** The Great Wall is a world famous tourist destination, attracting a large _____ of tourists from home and abroad every year.

**10** In some regions, wind can be exploited to _____ electricity.

| boost | equality | tackle | fade | alarming |
| literate | track | perspective | creative | campaign |

1 All other issues _____ into insignificance compared with the struggle for survival.

2 We did all we could to inspire his _____ thinking, expecting that he could think up some new ideas for the project.

3 The industrial revolution at first needed large quantities of unskilled workers; but as it developed, there was a growing need for the workforce to be _____.

4 Lower interest rates can _____ the economy by reducing borrowing costs for consumers and businesses.

5 You can use this app to keep _____ of your exercise progress.

6 The government is determined to _____ inflation and get the economy back on track.

7 She is leading a nationwide _____ against domestic violence.

8 The government must promote gender _____ because women deserve more opportunities.

9 Due to the rapid pace of urbanization, our countryside is disappearing at an _____ rate.

10 The experience of volunteering in the hospital has changed my _____ on life.

# DAY 17 练习

| accumulate | countless | boast | giants | outdated |
|---|---|---|---|---|
| annual | discipline | engage | exceeded | collective |

**1** The young man was fined because he had _____ the speed limit.

**2** People will often _____ about how many "friends" they may have in their real or online network.

**3** Technology, which has changed the life of _____ people, is the application of scientific knowledge.

**4** Tech _____ like Microsoft are attracted by the availability of clean energy to power their data centers.

**5** Social progress is by no means an individual effort, and it is always the result of _____ effort.

**6** According to a recent survey, only 15% of people would _____ in regular exercise.

**7** Our library should purchase updated books to replace the _____ ones.

**8** The _____ of studying music can help children develop good work habits and improve self-esteem.

**9** Students can _____ working experience by doing part-time jobs.

**10** Retail stores usually count on the Christmas season to earn half of their _____ profits.

| | | | | |
|---|---|---|---|---|
| attach | contract | perceived | symptom | slight |
| suspect | principal | definite | casual | implications |

**1** The police say they _____ the attack has been carried out by animal rights activists.

**2** The rise in inflation was just one _____ of the poor state of the economy.

**3** It is difficult to measure the social _____ of new and rapidly changing technologies.

**4** The construction company wins a federal _____ to build a new bridge.

**5** A _____ working attitude may lead to serious error in work.

**6** Stress is widely _____ as contributing to the occurrence heart disease.

**7** Even a _____ change in the price may be noticed by price-sensitive consumers.

**8** Parents always _____ great importance to their children's scores in school.

**9** When students leave school, they often do not have _____ plans for their future.

**10** In many parts of the world, renewable energy is already a _____ energy source.

# DAY 18 练习

| | | | | |
|---|---|---|---|---|
| excluded | fulfill | enforce | crash | approved |
| enroll | translated | prosperity | urgent | occur |

**1** Individuals can _____ on self-study programs in the university's language institute.

**2** When people lose their jobs, they may feel _____ from the work environment that offers purpose in life.

**3** There is a sign that the economy is recovering from the global _____.

**4** The government is taking some steps to address the _____ need for food and water in the disaster area.

**5** The country ensures that its economic growth is _____ into meaningful improvements for its citizens.

**6** He expects that his application for resignation will be _____ immediately.

**7** Our imitation of behaviors may _____ without our realizing it.

**8** Boulder was one of the first cities in the nation to _____ a ban on smoking.

**9** Many adults are unwilling to _____ their duty to take care of their elderly parents.

**10** While the economy in Japan begin to decline in 1990, US economy in 1991 entered the longest period of _____ in its history.

| enhance | legitimate | allowance | conditional | liberate |
| offend | scarce | shocking | profitable | intention |

**1** Machines can _____ people from boring daily tasks.

**2** According to the law, it is _____ to check suspects' phone contents.

**3** Formal suit can _____ the professional image of workers.

**4** He apologizes for his improper comments which _____ the public.

**5** It is _____ that so many cases of school bullying occur each year.

**6** While some people try to make a permanent home in the United States, others have no _____ to stay.

**7** The production of coffee beans is a huge, _____ business.

**8** Fresh food is so _____ that prices have rocketed.

**9** The unemployment benefit is not _____, and anyone losing jobs can claim it.

**10** He received a handsome _____ from his company to cover his business trip expenses.

# DAY 19 练习

| launched | prevailing | committing | grasp | investigate |
|----------|------------|------------|-------|-------------|
| pursuing | advocates | function | combine | dramatic |

**1** It seems that adults are constantly _____ true happiness.

**2** The student fails to _____ the opportunity to study abroad.

**3** Some people imagine the United States as a place where they can be productive for a while without _____ themselves to staying forever.

**4** The report _____ greater study of foreign languages and international affairs to meet the challenge of globalization.

**5** The serious drought is expected to have _____ effects on the California agriculture.

**6** Michelle Obama _____ a campaign against childhood obesity, even regarding it as the greatest national security threat.

**7** An independent body has been set up to _____ the accident.

**8** The main _____ of the investment banks is to raise capital for industry.

**9** There is a _____ view that smart phones have changed our communication patterns.

**10** In order to keep in good health, you should try to _____ regular exercise with a balanced diet.

| nevertheless | deserted | conserve | boom | joint |
| compared | feedback | proclaimed | clarity | heighten |

**1** As all villagers have migrated to cities, their village is _____.

**2** Living standards improved rapidly during the post-war _____.

**3** The campaign is intended to _____ public awareness of the white pollution.

**4** As many people hit middle age, they start to notice that their memory and mental _____ are not what they used to be.

**5** The new government set up its own army and _____ its independence.

**6** _____ efforts are needed in modern research, since it is impossible for a scientist to finish all projects.

**7** We need both positive and negative _____ from our customers.

**8** There is little chance that we will succeed in changing the law. _____, we should try.

**9** 22% of American college graduates now major in business _____ with only 2% in history.

**10** We should _____ oil and gas by making full use of other energy sources.

# DAY 20 练习

| procedure | embrace | reluctant | dispute | revive |
| --- | --- | --- | --- | --- |
| discard | presence | obtain | restrict | defeated |

**1** The two countries are in _____ over the boundaries of their coastal waters.

**2** Some people may suppose that they can _____ lasting satisfaction from the money spent.

**3** Without self-confidence, a person can be easily _____ by challenge.

**4** The company makes great effort to _____ its fading business.

**5** Americans are willing to tolerate time-consuming security _____ in airports in return for increased safety.

**6** The government decides to _____ advertising of products high in fat, salt or sugar, and limit sponsorship of sports events by fast-food producers such as McDonald's.

**7** Consumers often _____ their old items and buy new ones.

**8** College graduates are often _____ to accept low-paid jobs.

**9** The _____ of alien army in this region is regarded as invasion.

**10** Compared with elderly people, youths are more ready to _____ novel ideas.

| transform | decreased | multiple | bonus | universal |
| champions | monitor | immense | destructive | reshaped |

**1** Human activities can have _____ effects on animals' natural habitats.

**2** There are already many devices on the market that can _____ people's exercise progress.

**3** The metabolic rate is the speed at which our bodies _____ food into energy.

**4** Second World War has _____ the political and economic map of the world.

**5** Thanks to the economic development, the number of young people out of work has _____ in recent years.

**6** As a progressive, he always _____ political and economic reforms.

**7** Performance _____ can motivate employees to work harder.

**8** Today, because of public health campaigns, many people regularly brush their teeth _____ times a day.

**9** While different cultures have different moral standards, some standards are _____.

**10** He has to work overtime today, since there is still an _____ amount of work to be done.

# DAY 21 练习

| massive | screen | accuse | effected | targeted |
|---------|--------|--------|----------|----------|
| access | operational | ease | federal | contradicts |

**1** To support employment, nothing would be more important than ensuring that every citizen has _____ to post-high-school education.

**2** Although several fast-fashion companies have made efforts to reduce their impact on the environment, lasting change can only be _____ by the customers.

**3** To help homeless people towards independence, the _____ government must support job training programs, raise the minimum wage, and fund more low-cost housing.

**4** New survey shows that women as well as men have lower levels of stress at work than at home, which _____ traditional wisdom.

**5** In order to survive, the company tries to lower its _____ cost by all means.

**6** Having a sense of humour is very important because it can _____ the tension between people.

**7** The company has been _____ by animal rights groups for its use of dogs in drugs trials.

**8** Traditional farming methods depend on _____ amounts of harmful chemicals.

**9** The manager will _____ suitable workers from all applicants to make sure they are competent for the job.

**10** Villagers _____ the company of destroying their fields to expand the banana plantations.

| profound | illustrate | accustom | ethical | collapse |
| permission | disrupted | supervise | outweigh | extensive |

**1** Bus services will be _____ tomorrow because of the bridge closure.

**2** It may take a while for freshmen to _____ themselves to new campus life.

**3** Examples are often used to _____ authors' point.

**4** Scientists carried out _____ research into renewable energy sources, ranging from wind energy to solar power.

**5** It seems that advantages of tourism largely _____ its disadvantages.

**6** Many fairy tales have _____ meanings, and they're not intended for children only.

**7** It is illegal to reproduce these books without _____ from the publisher.

**8** Researches involving human genes may involve some _____ issues.

**9** Two engineers were sent to a large telephone-parts factory to _____ a series of industrial experiments.

**10** His business empire is likely to _____ under a massive burden of debt.

# DAY 22 练习

| | | | | |
|---|---|---|---|---|
| crucial | promising | grant | cultivate | precious |
| response | principles | numerous | candidates | address |

**1** _____ of the Constitution should never be violated.

**2** _____ rivers, once the source of human prosperity and rich wildlife, are now heavily polluted.

**3** More innovative courses are being developed in order to _____ students' creativity.

**4** Most of employers are planning to cut down on wages instead of laying off employees in _____ to the economic depression.

**5** To ensure the future of mankind, it is _____ to draw on our experience from the past.

**6** In fact, we have already taken measures to _____ the issue of white pollution.

**7** Clean water is a _____ commodity in drought region of the world.

**8** The idea seems to be _____, but it is difficult to put it into practice.

**9** Fathers tend to _____ more independence to their children than mothers do.

**10** There were a large number of _____ for the job.

| property | cater | modify | permanent | distort |
| accessible | impairs | renewable | inevitable | tend |

**1** Failure is an _____ part of life, and we need to learn how to live with it.

**2** A reporter should be objective in his reporting rather than _____ the reality.

**3** While coal, oil and gas still generate about 85 percent of the world's energy supply, it's clear that the future belongs to _____ sources such as wind and solar power.

**4** Due to lower cost of production, smart phones are easily _____ to the general public.

**5** People who suffer from obesity must _____ their diets.

**6** According to the law, when couples get divorced, jointly acquired _____ should be divided equally.

**7** Consumption of alcohol _____ people's ability to drive a car or operate machinery.

**8** The creation by a great artist is an achievement as _____ as the discovery by a great scientist.

**9** In the contemporary western world, rapidly changing styles _____ to a desire for novelty and individualism.

**10** A large number of doctors and nurses are needed to _____ wounded soldiers.

# DAY 23 练习

| | | | | |
|---|---|---|---|---|
| intellectual | interfere | inclined | obligation | dismiss |
| attain | specific | subject | reveals | content |

**1** Some parents would _____ their children's dreams as worthless and force them to give up their dreams.

**2** It is impossible for us to _____ valuable information from free online resources.

**3** Mass media are _____ to cover disasters and deaths to draw the public attention.

**4** The new research _____ that by the third generation, the original language is lost in the majority of immigrant families.

**5** While parents are _____ with a stable lifestyle, young generations tend to value adventures and challenges.

**6** The study of law has been recognized for centuries as a basic _____ discipline in European universities.

**7** In order to achieve objectivity, reporters should never allow personal feelings to _____ with their reporting.

**8** Making _____ daily plans can help people increase their working efficiency.

**9** Constant tests _____ students to greater mental stress.

**10** We have a moral _____ to take good care of our aged parents.

| foresight | review | internal | delete | degrade |
| register | scheme | exception | pursuit | oriented |

**1** As people become older, their memory begin to _____.

**2** Any attempt to discuss the issue of human rights was rejected as an interference in the country's _____ affairs.

**3** No one have enough _____ to predict the economic crisis.

**4** The _____ has been set up to help homeless people.

**5** Most of the buildings in the town are modern, but the old church is an _____.

**6** A worker's quitting may be inspired by the _____ of new career goal.

**7** The government decides to conduct a thorough _____ of its economic policy.

**8** Owing to the current exam-_____ educational system, students attach much importance to their scores.

**9** When writing papers, you must _____ material that is unrelated to your thesis and add material necessary to illustrate your points.

**10** The online library provides an easy access to its resources to readers who _____ this service.

# DAY 24 练习

| | | | | |
|---|---|---|---|---|
| assumption | priority | arrest | endured | rigid |
| stimulated | witnessed | navigate | licence | provisions |

**1** Negative attitudes toward obesity have _____ a number of anti-obesity policies.

**2** Recent years have _____ a growing demand for private vehicles.

**3** Compared with other environmental issues, white pollution can hardly _____ the public attention.

**4** Fossil record shows that many species have _____ for millions of years.

**5** France and other countries have established legally binding _____ on placing women in top business positions.

**6** Without the aid of maps, ancient voyagers had to _____ by the stars.

**7** Due to shortage of laborers, requirements became less _____ in the selection of workers.

**8** Compared with men, women are more likely to give _____ to child care and education.

**9** Some people object to using animals in medical research on the _____ that animals also have rights.

**10** It is required by law that a driving test be taken before a man gets a _____.

| routine | assess | confine | executive | distract |
|---------|--------|---------|-----------|----------|
| precise | bound | anticipate | recession | proportion |

**1** Although three months have passed, the witness can still recall _____ details of the accident.

**2** Parents worry that playing video games will _____ children's attention from their homework.

**3** The _____ of the population who are over retirement age has grown tremendously in the past few years.

**4** Traditional tests can _____ students' analytical and verbal skills but fail to measure creativity and practical knowledge.

**5** An insurance company engages in numerous aspects and will not _____ itself to one business.

**6** We are _____ to see some ups and downs along the road to success.

**7** Making exercise a part of your daily _____ will be beneficial to your fitness.

**8** The president of the United States is the _____ head of the government.

**9** Many workers lose their jobs due to the lengthy economic _____.

**10** We need someone who can _____ and respond to changes in the fashion industry.

# DAY 25 练习

| | | | | |
|---|---|---|---|---|
| relevant | inhabitants | initiative | exert | contends |
| aggressive | surpass | obesity | surrounded | ancient |

**1** Given the rapid development of technology, machines may _____ humans in intelligence in the future.

**2** There's no doubt that our friends _____ enormous influence on our behaviors.

**3** It seems that compared with modern people, _____ people were more experienced in handling flood.

**4** Your humor must be _____ to the audience and should help to show them that you understand their situation.

**5** A good salesperson has to be _____ in today's competitive market.

**6** The plan to develop rural areas is strongly opposed by local _____ who value the countryside.

**7** These kids are going to be _____ by computers — in their pockets, in their offices, in their homes — for the rest of their lives.

**8** In her new book *Join the Club*, the author _____ that peer pressure can also be a positive force.

**9** Highly standardized jobs tend to leave no room for individual _____ or creativity.

**10** The study also demonstrates a direct link between _____ and heart disease.

| lobby | compulsory | soften | terminate | qualify |
| perception | severe | valid | intuitive | evaluate |

**1** He believes that the study of history should be _____ rather than optional in school.

**2** The student has been informed that he doesn't _____ for the scholarship because of his poor academic performance.

**3** Our research attempts to _____ the effectiveness of different drugs.

**4** Measures have been taken to _____ the impact of the natural disaster on this region.

**5** The chief executive has _____ reasons for refusing to accept these proposals.

**6** The _____ group formed by tobacco company is trying to block government's efforts to ban smoking.

**7** Sometimes, executive will make decision based on their _____ sense rather than systematic analysis.

**8** In order to reduce cost, the company decides to _____ all corporate welfare programs.

**9** Parents often rely on _____ punishment to force their children follow certain rules.

**10** The _____ of our own strength and weakness is limited by our age.

# DAY 26 练习

| deceptive | conservative | evolved | chronic | delayed |
|-----------|--------------|---------|---------|---------|
| logical | refute | random | corporation | wander |

**1** Researchers have recruited 30 volunteers for the study and separated them into two groups at _____.

**2** Sensible ideas have been around for a long time, but the government is too _____ to put them into practice.

**3** The homeless _____ on the street, without any particular sense of purpose.

**4** Appearance can be _____, and we should not rely on looks to judge other people.

**5** There is no easy short-term solution to the country's _____ economic problems.

**6** The tiny company has _____ into a major chemical manufacturer.

**7** Due to unfavourable weather conditions, the launch of the rocket is _____.

**8** His argument is so robust that it is difficult to _____ it.

**9** In spite of the current world economic downturn, the transnational _____ is continuing with its investment plans in China.

**10** It is the philosophy that provides us with the power of _____ thinking.

| welfare | exercise | shift | fuels | democratic |
| consistent | tension | vanished | alternative | fashion |

**1** The jury system is an expression of crucial _____ values, including the principles that all citizens are equally competent to serve on juries.

**2** Owing to destruction of natural habitat, many species have _____ or are facing extinction.

**3** The _____ system may intensify people's dependence and laziness.

**4** While all of these countries face their own challenges, there are a number of _____ issues, such as global warming.

**5** In many countries, there has been a _____ of emphasis from manufacturing to service industries.

**6** The Court's decision _____ the debate over physician-assisted suicide.

**7** Governments _____ political and economic power to maintain social functioning.

**8** Eating at home is a realistic _____ to eating out.

**9** Arizona has attempted to _____ state policies that ran parallel to the existing federal ones.

**10** Smiling and laughing has actually been shown to relieve _____ and stress.

# DAY 27 练习

| | | | | |
|---|---|---|---|---|
| appeal | current | dominate | status | outlines |
| bias | convert | gender | remarkable | relatively |

**1** These findings suggest the elephants have built up a _____ capacity to make distinctions between human voices.

**2** During the hiring process, some companies still have a strong _____ against women.

**3** Handmade goods often _____ to those who are tired of industrial products.

**4** The article is actually quite optimistic, since it _____ a potential solution to this problem.

**5** Although a growing number of women go to work, men still _____ the job market.

**6** If people _____ the wetlands to farmland, birds will not have enough space to live.

**7** Lack of exercise is also a risk factor for heart disease but it's _____ small when compared with the others.

**8** The _____ state of affairs may have been fueled by the lack of legal penalty.

**9** Massive male unemployment has diminished the _____ of men in the family.

**10** The government must promote _____ equality because women deserve more opportunities.

| ambitious | vehicles | existing | minimize | finance |
| susceptible | sparked | upgraded | diligent | lessened |

**1** A healthy lifestyle can help people _____ the risk of developing cancer.

**2** Existing leisure facilities are worn-out in the town and need to be _____.

**3** Jeya feels that her _____ nature made her unsuitable for a humble position.

**4** Women are particularly _____ to depression and anxiety disorders compared to men.

**5** Physician-assisted suicide has _____ serious ethical controversies.

**6** _____ laws fail to keep pace with rapid social changes.

**7** Obviously, _____ workers tend to have higher working efficiency.

**8** The impact of climate change can be _____ by reducing future greenhouse gas emissions.

**9** Battery-powered _____ are replacing those that run on fossil fuel.

**10** The fund has been used largely to _____ the construction of a new school.

# DAY 28 练习

| | | | | |
|---|---|---|---|---|
| shrinking | integrate | abstract | devices | excessive |
| coordinate | ecology | virtue | harbor | popularize |

**1** Consumption of unhealthy food should be seen to be just as damaging as smoking or _____ drinking.

**2** Thanks to technological advancement, there are many electrical labour-saving _____ around the home.

**3** Wildfires have become a national concern because they have severely damaged the _____ of west area.

**4** Modesty is regarded as an important _____ in China.

**5** It is difficult for ordinary viewers to appreciate _____ art.

**6** Government officials visited the earthquake zone on Thursday morning to _____ the relief effort.

**7** Teachers, employers, and health professionals have been shown to _____ biases against the obese.

**8** The demand for new car is _____, as consumers temper their spending.

**9** Advertising is a common strategy used by companies to _____ their new products.

**10** Immigrants need to make great effort to _____ into local community.

| thrive | diminish | assume | widespread | costly |
| subscribe | immune | initially | rewarding | charity |

**1** Rational consumers are often _____ to the influence of advertisement.

**2** Many researchers _____ that many children's views on real world are influenced by the media.

**3** New evidence suggests that our memory may not _____ with age.

**4** The plan receives _____ support throughout the country, since it will create thousands of new job opportunities.

**5** It is rather _____ to install the purification system, but it will pay off in the long run.

**6** Buying gifts for others or donating money to _____ is often more pleasurable than purchasing things for oneself.

**7** The process of acquiring a new skill may be frustrating, but it can be _____.

**8** Some plants can grow and _____ in extreme environment.

**9** The death toll in the earthquake was _____ reported at around 250, but was later revised to 300.

**10** Many economists _____ to this theory, but many politicians dismiss it as a nonsense.

# DAY 29 练习

| | | | | |
|---|---|---|---|---|
| isolated | slimmed | underestimate | prospect | agency |
| wears | mature | sacrifice | highlight | subsidy |

**1** The jobless try to seek _____ from the local government.

**2** None of us should ever _____ the degree of difficulty women face in career advancement.

**3** When writing a resume, you need to _____ your working experience and accomplishment.

**4** Conservative investors tend to prefer _____ industries rather than infant ones.

**5** Patients will be _____ from other people for one month after treatment.

**6** He is delighted at the _____ of studying abroad.

**7** We don't have to _____ environmental protection to promote economic growth.

**8** The government has to create a special _____ to address the need of homeless people.

**9** The company has recently _____ its product line in response to lower demand.

**10** For many people downshifting is merely a fashion, and the novelty soon _____ off.

| skeptical | eliminate | rivals | respects | traffic |
| prone | features | adventure | imitate | modest |

**1** Tired drivers are found to be particularly _____ to ignore warning signs along the road.

**2** No computer can _____ the complex functions of the human brain.

**3** The area is famous for its wonderfully fragrant wine which has no _____ in the world.

**4** Extreme sports can satisfy the need of people who have a strong sense of _____.

**5** Although Jack has made full preparations for the match, he is still _____ about his chance of winning.

**6** In many _____, immigrants have been successfully absorbed into the local society.

**7** Website with strong _____ can attract advertisers to place their content on the website.

**8** It's a great film and it _____ a Spanish actor who is going to be a world star within a year.

**9** If the school finds that homework is unimportant to its students' academic achievement, it should reduce or _____ the assignments.

**10** Due to the weak market, there was only a _____ increase in the sales volume.

# DAY 30 练习

| grounds | collaborate | owes | strive | extinct |
|---------|-------------|------|--------|---------|
| infinite | rational | strategy | inferior | correspond |

**1** The case was dismissed on the _____ that there was not enough evidence.

**2** He _____ his failure to lack of willpower.

**3** The _____ distances of space are too great for the human mind to grasp.

**4** At the current rate of decline, many of the rain forest animals could become _____ in less than 10 years.

**5** We should not _____ merely for quantity of production. Instead, we must pursue excellence.

**6** The decision was based on emotion rather than _____ thought.

**7** In many markets, _____ products can act as partial substitutes for more costly superior products.

**8** Researchers around the world need to _____ in order to develop a new vaccine against the epidemic.

**9** The company plans to sponsor television programs as part of its marketing _____.

**10** Actually, all of us desire to achieve success, but sometimes our actions don't _____ with what we desire.

| guidelines | elite | inherent | lengthy | absence |
| participate | alter | disorder | substitute | fruitful |

**1** If you have no friends, try to _____ in several online communities, where people are always willing to share advice and encouragement.

**2** An unauthorized hacker is able to access a computer database and to _____ information stored there.

**3** The medical community has drawn up _____ on the treatment of the dying patients.

**4** Devoted concertgoers insist that recordings are no _____ for live performance.

**5** These steps prove so _____ that the company has expanded its market share.

**6** Repetitive and _____ explanations may not impress students, but most likely will turn them off.

**7** The _____ of any women on the board of directors reflects the gender imbalance in the business world.

**8** French doctors tend to regard drug dependence as a form of deep-rooted psychological _____.

**9** Humans have an _____ need to socialize with others.

**10** Public opinion can be influenced by small _____ groups who control the media.

# 第四部分

## 80+必备学术词汇配套练习

### DAY 31 练习

| | | | | |
|---|---|---|---|---|
| plausible | dilemma | counterparts | absurd | infrastructures |
| successive | constraints | integrity | ambiguous | contempt |

**1** Governments have made _____ efforts to get out of the lengthy economic depression.

**2** The idea sounds _____ on the whole, although there are some logical errors.

**3** Far more Japanese workers expressed dissatisfaction with their jobs than did their _____ in the 10 other countries surveyed.

**4** This looks like an _____ story, but similar stories happen at all time in the real world.

**5** They decide to abandon their trip because of financial _____.

**6** Building _____, such as roads or railways, will contribute to the economy.

**7** Justices show a _____ for the misdeed of some politicians.

**8** The public feel confused about the _____ statement made by the local government.

**9** In an era of growing criticism against politicians, Mr. Mandela is a model of honesty and _____.

**10** He was faced with the _____ of whether or not to study abroad.

| predominant | deprive | opponent | impartial | exaggerate |
|---|---|---|---|---|
| unparalleled | evaporated | assembling | squeeze | intricate |

**1** Life is tough, and we need to _____ as much pleasure from each day as we possibly could.

**2** Too many parents focus on their children's academic performance. But in doing so, they also _____ their children of happiness.

**3** It is a mistake to underestimate your _____ in the race.

**4** As we are running out of traditional energy, the electric vehicle may become a _____ choice in the future.

**5** The Renaissance was an epoch of _____ cultural achievement.

**6** Some environmentalists tend to _____ the extent of climate change in order to draw the public attention.

**7** The job security that the US economy once offered to high school graduates has largely _____.

**8** The factory makes profits by _____ parts for trucks.

**9** Justices should act in ways that strengthen the court's reputation for being independent and _____.

**10** Although the problem is _____, it can be solved very quickly with a computer.

# DAY 32 练习

| | | | | |
|---|---|---|---|---|
| conceives | acclaim | overestimate | astonishing | vocational |
| supplement | intervention | paradox | prompted | insidious |

**1** Without proper _____, school bullying will get worse.

**2** He _____ the idea of transforming the old power station into an arts centre.

**3** It is a curious _____ that professional comedians often have unhappy personal lives.

**4** Malaria is an _____ disease that may go unnoticed.

**5** The writer has received much _____ and yet he often considers himself a failure.

**6** His ability to absorb information was _____, but his concentration span was short.

**7** Japan's recession has _____ consumers to cut back on buying cars.

**8** Some people do extra jobs outside their regular jobs to _____ their incomes.

**9** Generally, _____ schools should do a better job of developing students' problem-solving skills.

**10** Research finds that men often _____ their own contribution to domestic responsibilities and underestimate that of their wives.

| frugal | stagnation | reckless | curb | margins |
|--------|-----------|----------|------|---------|
| trivial | attribute | explicit | resent | discern |

**1** Be patient. Don't lose your temper over _____ matters.

**2** A range of policies have been introduced to _____ the inflation.

**3** Environmentalists _____ the idea that economic development should be given priority over environmental protection.

**4** Economic depression puts a necessary end to an era of _____ personal spending.

**5** Wise investors can _____ opportunities from plenty of options.

**6** The honourable worker lives a very _____ life and yet gives away most of his money to charities.

**7** People tend to _____ their success to external causes such as luck.

**8** Lengthy periods of economic _____ or decline have almost always left society more mean-spirited and less inclusive.

**9** Fixed-line telephones have played an important role in the past, but for the moment, they're on the _____.

**10** Compared with his conservative rivals, he is _____ about his intention to win the race.

# DAY 33 练习

| | | | | |
|---|---|---|---|---|
| impose | accountable | conceal | resist | aggravate |
| vulnerable | inconceivable | hypothesis | overwhelmed | indispensable |

**1** Grown-ups learn to _____ rather than express their emotions, in the workplace, in social settings, and at home.

**2** The new tax system will _____ additional financial burdens on many workers.

**3** People with high blood pressure are especially _____ to diabetes.

**4** Well-paid executives should be _____ for what happens in the organizations that they run.

**5** It is difficult for teenagers to _____ the temptation of online games.

**6** The double-digit inflation will certainly _____ the current economic situation.

**7** A good dictionary is _____ for learning a foreign language.

**8** It is _____ that some officials are not aware of the seriousness of crime in this region.

**9** The scientific method requires testing a proposed scientific _____ before accepting it as the truth.

**10** I never feel _____ with the amount of information my brain absorbs.

| acquisition | counterbalance | quota | eligible | mandates |
|---|---|---|---|---|
| privilege | speculate | discriminate | resembles | controversial |

**1** Workers use their leisure time to _____ the mental tension brought by jobs.

**2** It is illegal for employers to _____ employees on grounds of race, sex or religion.

**3** As a member of the nobility, his life had been one of wealth and _____.

**4** Although American society _____ European society in many ways, it has a character that is distinctly different.

**5** The gender-balance bill would force employers to adopt a _____ system when recruiting female workers.

**6** Professionalism has turned the _____ of a doctoral degree into a must for a successful academic career.

**7** This strange signal has led scientists to _____ on the existence of life on other planets.

**8** This is a _____ policy which has attracted widespread criticism.

**9** Only the unemployed are _____ for this special benefit.

**10** This district has produced a policy which _____ that homework should not account for more than 10% of a student's academic grade.

# DAY 34 练习

| | | | | |
|---|---|---|---|---|
| identical | consensus | penalty | transparent | comply |
| contemplate | transient | foreshadow | incentive | overrule |

**1** _____ investors, who demand fast returns from companies, can harm a firm's efforts to invest in long-term development.

**2** So long as there is a demand for these drugs, the financial _____ for drug dealers will be there.

**3** The two pictures are similar, although not _____.

**4** Consumer advocates say all operators need to be more _____ about the cost of mobile bandwidth.

**5** The Supreme Court decides to _____ controversial proposals.

**6** There is a general _____ among teachers about the need for greater security in schools.

**7** Rational consumers tend to _____ for a long time before buying.

**8** ObamaCare requires large employers to offer health insurance to workers, or they will face a _____.

**9** The company is fined, because it has failed to _____ with environmental regulations.

**10** Declining house prices in the capital _____ a weakening housing market in the rest of Britain.

| overturns | disproportionately | offset | verify | foster |
| transition | conform | underlined | looming | monopoly |

**1** We need to ensure a smooth _____ from the old system to the new one.

**2** The report has _____ the need to develop renewable energy to address energy crisis.

**3** Developed countries have a responsibility to _____ global economic growth to help emerging countries.

**4** By virtue of its superb products, the company has a virtual _____ in the market.

**5** The company has raised the price of products in order to _____ the increased cost of materials.

**6** Smoking poses a _____ threat to our physical fitness.

**7** The unemployed often lack safety nets, and suffer _____ in times of economic hardship.

**8** Due to lack of sufficient evidence, the Court _____ the conviction.

**9** She was not an accountant and didn't have the expertise to _____ the accuracy of these financial details.

**10** Tourists are supposed to _____ to the local customs.

# DAY 35 练习

| | | | | |
|---|---|---|---|---|
| aggregate | liability | status quo | fatal | worship |
| counteract | scrutinize | humiliated | undermined | compromise |

**1** The report reveals _____ flaws in security procedure at the airport.

**2** Positive emotions bring us pleasure, _____ the damaging effects of negative emotions, and promote long-term physical and emotional health.

**3** Researchers _____ available data to make a prediction concerning the economic situation.

**4** A growing number of teenagers begin to _____ and even copy their idols.

**5** After failing in the election campaign, the candidate feels _____.

**6** The man is so stubborn that he refuses to make any _____ in his standpoint.

**7** Our confidence in the team has been seriously _____ by their recent defeats.

**8** The conservative party refuses to make changes and tries to maintain the _____.

**9** The insurance company does not assume _____ for any damage caused by natural disasters.

**10** On behalf of shareholders, boards will _____ every project that concerns the growth of the company.

| unanimous | reinforces | uplifting | intrigued | sanctions |
|-----------|-----------|-----------|-----------|-----------|
| flawed | sponsor | conviction | sarcastic | concrete |

**1** The company plans to _____ television programs as part of its marketing strategy.

**2** The strong desire to make a fortune _____ his dream of starting his own business.

**3** We are delighted to hear the _____ news that our team have won in the race.

**4** Member countries that do not obey rules established by EU will face _____.

**5** _____ evidence is needed to prove this new theory.

**6** Many economists argue that GDP is a _____ concept, since it measures things that do not matter and misses things that do.

**7** Due to lack of sufficient evidence, the US Supreme Court has overturned the corruption _____ of a former Virginia governor.

**8** Although the plan received _____ approval, this does not mean that it is perfect.

**9** The complex story line in the book has _____ countless readers.

**10** The insensitive teachers often pokes fun at students' shortcomings with _____ remarks.

# DAY 36 练习

| | | | | |
|---|---|---|---|---|
| dwarfed | blunder | augment | adhere | obsessed |
| endorse | sentiment | overshadows | facilitate | bizarre |

**1** Most scholars seem to _____ this viewpoint for its reasonableness.

**2** Smart phones _____ our communication by offering a wide range of new communication patterns.

**3** In order to _____ the family income, he is doing several part-time jobs.

**4** The massive leakage of customers' information _____ the information security system of the company.

**5** Younger and less experienced managers are more likely to be influenced by their _____.

**6** All members of the association should _____ to a strict code of practice.

**7** Consumers tend to be _____ with scarce products.

**8** It is _____ that wealthy aristocratic families should still be the symbolic heart of modern democratic states.

**9** The old houses were _____ by the huge new tower blocks.

**10** While some in the company welcome the new marketing strategy, others regard it as a huge potential _____.

| onerous | erase | dearth | implement | embody |
|---------|-------|--------|-----------|--------|
| indulgent | zealous | inherit | cement | hostile |

**1** According to the law, it is his son that will _____ his possessions after he dies.

**2** They are desperate to _____ the painful memory of that last defeat.

**3** The _____ of moral principles will lead to social disorders.

**4** Designs on the flag are intended to _____ the spirit of our nation.

**5** She is a _____ worker for charity, devoting herself to charitable causes.

**6** Sensible policies have been around for a long time, but the government has been too conservative to _____ them.

**7** Bringing up a child is an _____ task for young parents.

**8** The dry climate condition is _____ for plants to grow.

**9** His _____ mother was willing to let him do anything he wanted.

**10** The president's visit was intended to _____ the alliance between the two countries.

# DAY 37 练习

| | | | | |
|---|---|---|---|---|
| demise | impressionable | steady | heritage | genuine |
| scatter | rigorous | compliment | confront | bureaucratic |

**1** In order to become qualified teachers, candidates must pass _____ assessments.

**2** Despite the predictions of their _____, minority languages still thrive in some regions.

**3** Traditional festivals are also part of precious cultural _____ that is passed down from our ancestors.

**4** We must learn how to _____ unexpected failures with optimism.

**5** Fake luxury watches are sold at a fraction of the price of the _____ ones.

**6** Elected politicians must be allowed to help their supporters deal with _____ problems.

**7** Indeed we have seen a _____ rise in the number of graduates flooding into the labor market.

**8** When others pay a unique _____ to your achievements, remain humble.

**9** Farmers _____ the seeds over the land, expecting a good harvest in autumn.

**10** _____ teenagers are more likely to believe what their idols say.

| disposable | intimidate | distressed | oppressive | detrimental |
| cumbersome | retrospect | geared | benefactors | drastic |

**1** Although the computer system looks _____, it is actually easy to use.

**2** Children will become increasingly _____ if parents pay no attention to their needs.

**3** Many foods prove to be _____ to health because of the chemicals and additives they contain.

**4** Foreign food aid has led to a _____ reduction in the numbers of people dying of starvation.

**5** The candidate was accused of using illegal ways to _____ people into voting for him.

**6** In _____, child rearing is anything but a completely fulfilling and life-enriching experience.

**7** There is an _____ ideology that demands that parents should always be interacting with their children.

**8** The use of _____ products is considered ecologically unsound.

**9** These _____ have succeeded in their chosen fields, and they want to use their wealth to reward those who contribute significantly to science.

**10** The course has been _____ towards the specific needs of students.

# DAY 38 练习

| | | | | |
|---|---|---|---|---|
| incorporate | deliberate | extravagant | fragile | ironic |
| suppress | nonsense | grieve | obscure | comprised |

**1** As we grow up, we learn to control our emotions and even _____ them so that they are manageable and don't dictate our behaviors.

**2** Oil pollution could damage the _____ ecology of the coral reefs.

**3** The committee is _____ of representatives from both the public and private sectors.

**4** Life is not a bed of roses. We often _____ over various kinds of loss: a friendship, a romantic relationship or a house.

**5** Many smokers dismiss warnings about dangers of smoking as complete _____.

**6** We mustn't let these minor details _____ the main issue.

**7** Several car manufacturers _____ the new control systems into their vehicles.

**8** It is _____ that so many women are anti-feminist.

**9** Fantasies of great wealth often involve visions of fancy cars and _____ homes.

**10** The debate over whether graffiti is art or _____ damage is still going on.

| impulsive | retreat | compel | alleviated | mighty |
|-----------|---------|--------|------------|--------|
| permeate | infringe | hinder | thorny | impoverish |

**1** To copy these materials without permission from the publisher is to _____ copyright.

**2** _____ spending is not a wise option, especially during the economic depression.

**3** The company is regarded as a _____ rival by competitors for its predominance in the market.

**4** Some diseases beat a _____ in face of medical advancement.

**5** Automation may _____ countless middle-class families by replacing human workers.

**6** The coming use of autonomous vehicles will pose many _____ ethical questions.

**7** Toyota Motor _____ some of the damage from its recall crisis earlier this year with a relatively quick social-media response campaign.

**8** The Europe Union is now considering legislation to _____ corporate boards to maintain a certain proportion of women   up to 60 percent.

**9** A gap year does not _____ the success of academic pursuits; in fact, it probably enhances it.

**10** American literature, movies, and music _____ foreign societies — especially appealing to young people in those societies.

# DAY 39 练习

| | | | | |
|---|---|---|---|---|
| comprehensive | yielded | backfire | aftermath | induce |
| fabricate | reckon | assimilate | transferred | instinctive |

**1** It is important to remember that we shouldn't try too hard to be happy. Scientists tell us this can _____ and actually have a negative impact on our well-being.

**2** New arrivals find it hard to _____ themselves into the local community.

**3** Due to his good performance in work, he is _____ from the sales department to human resource department.

**4** *The Rough Guide to Nepal* is a _____ guide to the region, including all important aspects concerning this country.

**5** Economists _____ 40% jobs will disappear in current economic downturn.

**6** Some irresponsible reporters may _____ sensational stories to arrest the public attention.

**7** The governor has _____ to the lobby pressure and approves the new tax plan.

**8** Unlike more complex feelings, fear is _____, and requires no conscious thought.

**9** The low price of electric cars is attractive enough to _____ consumers to abandon traditional cars.

**10** In the _____ of the recession, people become less materialistic and more financially prudent.

| elevate | elaborate | pessimistic | asset | fluctuate |
|---------|-----------|-------------|-------|-----------|
| prudent | intimate | deteriorates | illusory | setback |

**1** The privacy of customers is a valuable _____ which needs to be guarded by companies.

**2** The team suffered a major _____ when their best player was injured in the race.

**3** It is natural for us to feel _____ after continuous failures.

**4** Compared with younger managers, experienced executives tend to be more _____ in taking actions.

**5** To maintain a mysterious air, the spokesman refused to _____ on the functions of this new car.

**6** Due to shortage of frequent interactions, we're not on _____ terms with our neighbors.

**7** People tend to have _____ superiority. For instance, 90% of us rate ourselves as above average in driving.

**8** This was an attempt to _____ football to a subject worthy of serious study.

**9** The discussion between two parties quickly _____ into an angry argument.

**10** During the crisis, oil prices tend to _____ between $20 and $40 a barrel.

# DAY 40 练习

| | | | | |
|---|---|---|---|---|
| resistant | precede | transmit | eradicate | assert |
| devastate | renaissance | default | invalidate | exclusive |

**1** The change in climate is leading to more frequent wildfires, which could _____ the region's ecosystems.

**2** According to a survey, most users stick with _____ settings on their computers, and they never modify them.

**3** We have developed the necessary agro-technological tools to _____ hunger, from genetically engineered crops to artificial fertilizers.

**4** Many lawyers _____ that the bill violates the First Amendment.

**5** We have to admit that a successful career and family life can be mutually _____.

**6** The more pesticides are used, the more _____ the insects will become, so more pesticides have to be used, which is a vicious circle.

**7** Mosquitoes can _____ certain diseases to humans.

**8** According to the Constitution, federal laws _____ state laws.

**9** The White House claims that it could _____ any controversial state law that it disagrees with.

**10** Popular art is experiencing a _____, attracting a growing number of followers.

| gloom | hierarchical | refrain | flourish | radical |
|-------|--------------|---------|----------|---------|
| peculiar | possessions | cap | substantial | context |

**1** People have lost their homes and all their _____ in the earthquake.

**2** _____ social reforms are needed to help the country get rid of poverty completely.

**3** There was a feeling of _____ and depression in the office when the news of the job cuts was announced.

**4** Few businesses _____ in the present economic downturn.

**5** This geographic condition is _____ to the region and cannot be found anywhere else.

**6** Reporters aim to be objective in their writing, but they cannot escape the _____ of their unique life experiences.

**7** In order to reduce unnecessary expenditure, the government has placed a _____ on local council spending.

**8** We should decrease our emphasis on celebrity gossip and _____ from displaying such stories on our magazine covers.

**9** A _____ number of mothers with young children are deterred from undertaking paid work because they lack access to childcare.

**10** Some royal family members have both an expensive taste of lifestyle and a pretty _____ view of the world.

# DAY 41 练习

| | | | | |
|---|---|---|---|---|
| determine | uncover | instrument | forecasts | instances |
| assigned | materials | poisonous | dispose | counts |

**1** It is necessary to _____ of nuclear waste for environmental safety.

**2** The professor _____ a challenging research project to each student.

**3** The research is intended to _____ the origin of Hawaiian culture.

**4** We have accumulated enough experience to make evidence-based _____ about the future.

**5** Eco-friendly _____ were employed in building the house.

**6** The Internet can be used as an ideal _____ of learning.

**7** Scientists are trying to _____ the causes of disease.

**8** Industrial waste is even more harmful since there are many highly _____ materials in it, such as copper and lead.

**9** The book provides many _____ of how to apply this theory in practice.

**10** It doesn't matter where charities get their money from; what _____ is what they do with it.

| originate | inquire | expenditure | superficial | bankrupt |
| accidental | derives | extended | appointed | nutrition |

**1** The hidden sadness and depression found in the artist's paintings _____ from his unhappy childhood.

**2** The human body requires a balanced diet to maintain good _____.

**3** The demand for higher education _____ to social classes that had not thought of attending a university before the war.

**4** The team's victory was _____, as it had not been expected to win.

**5** A committee was appointed to _____ into the cause of the forest fire.

**6** The book provides only a _____ overview of the topic and fails to consider the deeper issues.

**7** His art is inspired by the natural world, from which he _____ much of his subject matter.

**8** The company's _____ on research and development has exceeded its revenue.

**9** The company went _____ because of poor management and inability to diversify its products.

**10** The journal has _____ seven experts to check statistical errors in papers to be published.

# DAY 42 练习

| | | | | |
|---|---|---|---|---|
| financial | mindful | regulate | ordinary | detailed |
| privacy | resourceful | damage | creatures | retain |

**1** He had always been fascinated by the _____ that lived in the ocean, and he spent years studying them.

**2** The company is experiencing _____ difficulties due to the economic downturn.

**3** Long-term exposure to noise can cause serious _____ to the hearing.

**4** _____ people can achieve extraordinary things when they set their minds to it and work towards their goals with determination.

**5** Individuals who are _____ and sophisticated are more likely to achieve success in their careers.

**6** It's important to be _____ of our thoughts and actions, as they can have a significant impact on our lives.

**7** The ability to _____ emotion when confronted by stress is one of the most important of all life's skills.

**8** The report provides a _____ analysis of the market trends.

**9** The most basic reason why dialects should be preserved is that language helps to _____ a culture.

**10** Americans should take steps to protect their digital _____.

| | | | | |
|---|---|---|---|---|
| cooperate | conclusive | characteristic | innovation | tempted |
| unfamiliar | reputation | advance | worthwhile | complain |

**1** The restaurant has a _____ for serving the best food in town.

**2** His paintings are known for their bright colors and bold brushstrokes, which are _____ of his style.

**3** Their latest _____, which has the potential to revolutionize the industry, is the result of years of research and development.

**4** Spending time with family and friends is always _____, even if it means sacrificing other activities.

**5** International organizations are calling on countries to _____ to address global climate change.

**6** While studies have shown that acrylamide can cause neurological damage in mice, there is no _____ evidence that it causes cancer in humans.

**7** They were _____ to take a risk and invest all their money in the stock market, but they decided to play it safe.

**8** People often _____ that plastics are everywhere and don't break down easily.

**9** If you are _____ with words or idioms, you guess at their meaning, using clues presented in the context.

**10** With each _____ in the IT revolution, the best jobs will require workers to have better education to make themselves above average.

# DAY 43 练习

| | | | | |
|---|---|---|---|---|
| advisable | schedule | overcome | structure | landscape |
| weighed | devised | persuasive | coincidence | passionate |

**1** The lawyer used _____ techniques to convince the jury of his client's innocence.

**2** Understanding the chemical _____ of DNA was a major breakthrough in biology.

**3** Given the current economic climate, it is not _____ to invest all your savings in the stock market.

**4** He is a _____ advocate for animal rights and opposes the use of animals in medical research.

**5** The doctor _____ the risks and benefits of the surgery before recommending it.

**6** With the support of his friends, he was able to _____ his depression.

**7** It's not a _____ that airlines across the globe integrate various shades of blue in their cabin seats.

**8** The _____ of the rainforest is lush and green, home to a diverse array of plant and animal life.

**9** The government has _____ a new scheme to reduce the unemployment rate.

**10** The company has a flexible _____ for the employees, so they can work from home.

| | | | | |
|---|---|---|---|---|
| enlightened | competent | insurance | switch | fortunate |
| incident | deceive | relief | decorated | shields |

**1** The company _____ the consumers by hiding the truth about their flawed products.

**2** The more _____ a person is, the more likely they are to succeed in their chosen field.

**3** The ozone layer _____ the earth from the sun's ultraviolet rays.

**4** It is _____ for them to have escaped the accident with only minor injuries.

**5** The government launched an investigation into the _____ to ensure public safety.

**6** The article "Why We Sleep" by Matthew Walker _____ me on the importance of getting enough sleep for optimal health and performance.

**7** She _____ the room with flowers to create a romantic atmosphere.

**8** He breathed a sigh of _____ when he knew he had passed the important exam.

**9** Many students list one major on their college applications, but _____ to another after taking college classes.

**10** People need to get a full-time job that provides _____ in order to cover themselves and their families.

# DAY 44 练习

| | | | | |
|---|---|---|---|---|
| element | boundary | divided | belong | literature |
| feasible | contest | explosive | strike | emphasis |

**1** The plan sounds great but is not _____ in terms of technology.

**2** Education in the age of automation should put more _____ on creative potential.

**3** Doing regular exercise is an essential _____ in keeping healthy.

**4** As game becomes an increasingly important means in teaching, the _____ between study and playing has already been blurred.

**5** The _____ has been called off after the company agreed to meet some of the workers' demands.

**6** Classic _____ can help students understand different cultures and experiences.

**7** In a recent international _____ of reading ability for 15-year-olds, American students ranked 21st out of 34 countries.

**8** The study _____ undergraduates into two groups: some were advised to set out monthly goals and others were told to plan activities day by day.

**9** Individuals who _____ to the same social class tend to share common values.

**10** Sad to say, the moral decline of the younger generations may be a rather _____ situation in our modern society.

| | | | | |
|---|---|---|---|---|
| ingredients | disruptive | slack | consists | probe |
| clarify | thrill | endeavors | unprecedented | framework |

**1** The committee _____ of 10 members, representing different political parties and interest groups.

**2** Recent years have brought minority-owned businesses in the United States _____ opportunities as well as new risks.

**3** The beauty product contains several harmful _____ that can cause allergic reactions.

**4** The purpose of the present study was to _____ into the relationship between obesity and depression.

**5** The invention of the steam engine was a _____ technology that changed the traditional rules.

**6** The company issued a statement to _____ its position on the issue.

**7** She _____ to maintain a good relationship with her colleagues.

**8** The research _____ includes a literature review, data collection, and analysis.

**9** The economy has been suffering from _____ demand for goods and services.

**10** It gave me a big _____ to meet my favorite author in person.

# DAY 45 练习

| momentum | tighten | reserved | respectively | bothering |
|---|---|---|---|---|
| precaution | undertakes | circulate | thick | inspect |

**1** We are aware of the potential threats and have taken every _____.

**2** With the price increases, we are all having to _____ our belts.

**3** The company has _____ a large amount of money for research and development.

**4** The charity _____ initiatives to provide education and health care to children from disadvantaged families.

**5** The company's new product has gained _____ in the market and is becoming very popular.

**6** Unemployment rates in Canada and the United States were acceptable, at 3.5 per cent and 5.5 per cent _____.

**7** A number of companies use AI image processing technology to _____ infrastructure and prevent equipment failure or leaks before they happen.

**8** The noise was _____ me so much that I couldn't concentrate on my work.

**9** Rumors were already beginning to _____ that the project might have to be abandoned.

**10** The forest was _____ with trees, making it difficult to walk through.

| feeble | tentative | volatile | mechanism | detected |
| eminent | renders | alliance | restrain | illuminate |

**1** The project is still in a _____ phase and the final details have not been worked out yet.

**2** Some people believe that formal education tends to _____ students' minds and spirits rather than set them free.

**3** Instead of formulas and charts, the two instructors use games and drawings to _____ their main points.

**4** The company's _____ performance in the first quarter raised concerns among investors.

**5** Suffering is inevitable, but the courage to fight it _____ life worth living.

**6** The immune system is a complex _____ that protects the body from disease.

**7** The university has produced many _____ alumni in the fields of science and politics.

**8** The outbreak of swine flu that was first _____ in Mexico was declared a global epidemic on June 11, 2009.

**9** The two companies have formed an _____ to jointly develop a new product.

**10** The oil price is very _____ and can have a significant impact on the economy.

# DAY 46 练习

| coherent | withstand | turnover | threshold | underlie |
|----------|-----------|----------|-----------|----------|
| durable | sophisticated | portraits | spontaneous | dynamic |

**1** The furniture is made of high-quality, _____ wood that will last for generations.

**2** Even though humans have been upright for millions of years, our feet and back cannot easily _____ repeated strain imposed by oversize limbs.

**3** The museum has a collection of _____ of famous historical figures.

**4** The company's profit margin depends on its ability to control costs and increase _____.

**5** Human body is a _____ biological system and can renew itself constantly.

**6** Recent evidence suggests that communication systems of honeybees are more _____ than previously thought.

**7** The ideas in the paper are not _____ and lack a clear logical structure.

**8** With the development of photography, _____ smiles were relatively easy to capture by the 1890s.

**9** The factors which _____ the climate change are complex and not fully understood.

**10** As she graduated from college and stepped into the society, she was on the _____ of a new life.

| constrained | setting | vicious | encountered | swinging |
| overcharge | characterized | external | boycott | likelihood |

**1** Today many people find it difficult to trust their own opinion and tend to seek advice from _____ sources.

**2** The company's stock price has been _____ wildly in recent months.

**3** The energy company was found to _____ its customers for electricity.

**4** She _____ many difficulties when she first started her business.

**5** The process of scientific discovery is _____ by its uncertainty and complexity.

**6** The organization is calling on consumers to _____ goods from companies that use child labor.

**7** The unique _____ of the restaurant provides a romantic atmosphere for diners.

**8** Washing hand frequently and avoiding close contact with people who have colds can reduce the _____ of infection.

**9** When women strive for professional success, they are often _____ by family duties.

**10** The virus is _____ and can cause serious illness or death in some cases.

# DAY 47 练习

| pledged | liberal | consolidate | intensive | strain |
|---------|---------|-------------|-----------|--------|
| harsh | neutral | reverse | parallel | submit |

**1** A team of researchers working together in the laboratory would _____ the results of their research to a journal.

**2** Google has _____ not to design and develop AI-directed weapons that would violate international norms.

**3** The athlete is undergoing an _____ training program to prepare for the upcoming competition.

**4** The company is looking to _____ its position in the market by acquiring smaller competitors.

**5** The desert's _____ conditions made survival difficult for the early settlers.

**6** The company is trying to _____ its declining sales by launching a new product.

**7** The transport service cannot cope with the _____ of so many additional passengers.

**8** Arizona had attempted to fashion state policies that ran _____ to the existing federal ones.

**9** The government's _____ economic policies have encouraged foreign investment.

**10** The judge remained _____ throughout the trial and did not show any bias.

| manifest | stereotype | deficient | faint | sensible |
| captive | exemplify | foundation | sharpen | defensive |

**1** His success was built on a solid _____ of hard work and dedication.

**2** It is _____ to invest in education to improve one's career prospects.

**3** Since there are too much fake news on social media platforms, it is necessary for people to _____ their media litcracy skills.

**4** The research findings _____ the significant role of education in shaping an individual's future.

**5** We tend to become _____ when criticized by others.

**6** The _____ animals at the zoo were kept in small enclosures, without much space to move around.

**7** The soil in the area is _____ in nutrients, making it difficult to grow healthy crops.

**8** Her works _____ the principles of modern design, combining form and function.

**9** The _____ memory of her childhood faded away in her mind as she grew older.

**10** There is a _____ that vocational education is for kids who can't make it academically.

# DAY 48 练习

| | | | | |
|---|---|---|---|---|
| fracture | compassionate | punctual | ascertain | invasive |
| commemorate | hospitality | censorship | obedient | appetite |

**1** The organization is raising funds to build a memorial to _____ those who died in the war.

**2** His _____ for knowledge is insatiable, always seeking out new information and experience.

**3** The doctor was very _____ towards his patients, taking the time to listen to their concerns and fears.

**4** The government's _____ of the arts has sparked controversy and protests among artists and activists.

**5** The train is _____, arriving and departing on schedule without any delays.

**6** The company's financial statements revealed a _____ in their cash flow, raising concerns among investors.

**7** The city is known for its _____ and friendliness towards tourists.

**8** The child was _____ and well-behaved, always listening to his parents and doing what was expected of him.

**9** The company's marketing tactics are seen as too _____ since it tracks users' location and online activity.

**10** The scientists were able to _____ the cause of the disease after conducting extensive research.

| instantaneous | paralyze | disperse | insulate | extinguish |
| simultaneous | offensive | propagate | dreadful | prominent |

**1** This type of music is becoming increasingly acceptable to many who used to think it _____.

**2** The astronaut's spacesuit is designed to _____ him from the extreme conditions of space.

**3** She is a _____ figure in the world of fashion, known for her unique designs and style.

**4** Some hypotheses fail to account for _____ extinctions on land and in the seas.

**5** The fear of failure can _____ people's ability to take action.

**6** The conditions in the prison were _____, with overcrowding and poor sanitation.

**7** The company has taken emergency measures to _____ the crisis of data leakage and protect the privacy of customers.

**8** The force of the explosion was _____, destroying everything in the blink of an eye.

**9** The government is using various methods to _____ its policies on social media.

**10** The sun's rays began to _____ the clouds, revealing a blue sky.

# DAY 49 练习

| | | | | |
|---|---|---|---|---|
| imminent | trumpet | prosecuted | institution | corrupt |
| capture | representative | arbitrary | striking | brilliance |

**1** The company was _____ for fraud and environmental violations.

**2** The government is preparing for an _____ natural disaster.

**3** The company was able to _____ a large market share by offering high-quality products at affordable prices.

**4** The visual effects of the film were _____, leaving a lasting impression on the audience.

**5** The author's _____ in writing was evident in this amazing book.

**6** Although train operators _____ the improvements they have made, but passengers do not get a basic level of service.

**7** The museum is a cultural _____ that preserves and displays artifacts.

**8** Knowing as much relevant information as possible can help us avoid making _____ decisions.

**9** The police officer was fired for _____ behavior and abuse of power.

**10** The survey results are _____ of the opinions of the entire population.

| disintegrated | miserable | daunting | preaches | authentic |
|---|---|---|---|---|
| proceed | meddle | misinterpreted | saturated | disposition |

**1** Although humans are more intelligent, animals are more _____ in their behavior and responses than human beings.

**2** Her cheerful _____ makes her a pleasure to be around.

**3** The refugees were living in _____ conditions, with no access to clean water or proper shelter.

**4** The market is _____ with similar products, making it difficult for new entrants to gain a foothold.

**5** The company's board of directors does not _____ in the day-to-day operations of the business.

**6** The task of climbing Mount Qomolangma is a _____ challenge for even the most experienced mountaineers.

**7** The company decided to _____ with the acquisition, despite the initial resistance from the employees.

**8** The civil war _____ the country, causing widespread destruction and chaos.

**9** The novel's ending was _____ by many readers, leading to widespread confusion.

**10** The religious leader _____ about the importance of forgiveness and compassion, but some of his followers struggle to put these values into practice.

# DAY 50 练习

| | | | | |
|---|---|---|---|---|
| anonymous | nurture | magnitude | installed | dubious |
| spectacular | monarchy | complement | statistical | stiff |

**1** The company values employee feedback and strives to _____ a culture of innovation.

**2** The new therapy can be a useful technique to _____ traditional forms of psychotherapy.

**3** The management style was so _____ that it was difficult for the company to adjust its operations to new reality.

**4** The IT department _____ security software to protect the company's network.

**5** The scientist's discovery was _____, leading to a new treatment for cancer.

**6** The scientific discovery had a _____ that changed the way we think about the universe.

**7** The politician's ethics were called into question when he was caught in a _____ practice.

**8** The money was donated by a local businessman who wishes to remain _____.

**9** Most journals are weak in _____ review, and this damages the quality of what they publish.

**10** The _____, which is a special symbol of nationhood, is the oldest form of government in the world.

| | | | | |
|---|---|---|---|---|
| abdicate | apprehension | literally | forsakes | stern |
| substantiate | allegiance | lucrative | countermeasures | reconcile |

**1** It is hard for most people to _____ their career ambitions with family responsibilities.

**2** The researcher was able to _____ the effectiveness of the new treatment through controlled experiments.

**3** The bar exam is a truly _____ test for a would-be lawyer.

**4** The author's best-selling novel has made him one of the most _____ authors in the world.

**5** He _____ his old way of life and embraces a minimalist lifestyle.

**6** Some believe that the King should _____ in the face of growing public discontent.

**7** More emotional corporate vocabulary can infuse work with meaning and increase employees' _____ to the firm.

**8** The music was so loud that it _____ vibrated through my entire body.

**9** In response to the foreign trade sanctions, the government is implementing a series of _____.

**10** There is growing _____ that the surge in oil prices will bring about economic inflation.

# 附 录

## 参考答案

### DAY 1 答案

| | | | | |
|---|---|---|---|---|
| 1. applying | 2. optimistic | 3. sensitive | 4. Observe | 5. ceremony |
| 6. recommended | 7. check | 8. recognized | 9. solved | 10. embarrassed |

| | | | | |
|---|---|---|---|---|
| 1. assistance | 2. convey | 3. devoted | 4. mental | 5. accompanied |
| 6. various | 7. perform | 8. beneficial | 9. stressed | 10. tendency |

### DAY 2 答案

| | | | | |
|---|---|---|---|---|
| 1. stood | 2. promoted | 3. account | 4. recovered | 5. promise |
| 6. intends | 7. exact | 8. conduct | 9. deserve | 10. classified |

| | | | | |
|---|---|---|---|---|
| 1. expand | 2. admiration | 3. contribute | 4. accurate | 5. object |
| 6. generations | 7. spiritual | 8. exhibited | 9. talent | 10. techniques |

### DAY 3 答案

| | | | | |
|---|---|---|---|---|
| 1. achieve | 2. convince | 3. afford | 4. despite | 5. inform |
| 6. normal | 7. refuse | 8. guaranteed | 9. prove | 10. explore |

| | | | | |
|---|---|---|---|---|
| 1. bargains | 2. settle | 3. anxious | 4. claiming | 5. reduce |
| 6. essential | 7. acceptable | 8. restore | 9. facilities | 10. practical |

# DAY 4 答案

| 1. admit | 2. conflict | 3. acquired | 4. curious | 5. guilty |
|----------|-------------|-------------|------------|-----------|
| 6. raised | 7. comment | 8. selected | 9. puzzles | 10. offend |

| 1. reminded | 2. definition | 3. adapt | 4. signal | 5. chased |
|-------------|---------------|----------|-----------|-----------|
| 6. origin | 7. struggles | 8. create | 9. compensated | 10. depend |

# DAY 5 答案

| 1. declined | 2. adjusting | 3. addition | 4. inspire | 5. diverse |
|-------------|--------------|-------------|------------|------------|
| 6. attracted | 7. concentrate | 8. impressive | 9. barriers | 10. propose |

| 1. express | 2. abandon | 3. occasion | 4. aware | 5. gather |
|------------|------------|-------------|----------|-----------|
| 6. tough | 7. satisfied | 8. forgive | 9. criticized | 10. contact |

# DAY 6 答案

| 1. available | 2. purchase | 3. charge | 4. immediate | 5. exist |
|--------------|-------------|-----------|--------------|----------|
| 6. sufficient | 7. entertain | 8. attempts | 9. grateful | 10. confuse |

| 1. relieve | 2. apparent | 3. commercial | 4. confirmed | 5. expense |
|------------|-------------|---------------|--------------|------------|
| 6. secure | 7. adopt | 8. efficient | 9. exhausted | 10. frustrated |

# DAY 7 答案

| 1. stubborn | 2. request | 3. ignore | 4. predict | 5. approach |
|-------------|------------|-----------|------------|-------------|
| 6. blindly | 7. return | 8. desperate | 9. sympathy | 10. reflect |

| 1. delight | 2. wisdom | 3. require | 4. maintain | 5. defend |
| 6. constant | 7. Flexible | 8. imagine | 9. associate | 10. Occasionally |

## DAY 8 答案

| 1. persuaded | 2. organized | 3. replace | 4. prohibits | 5. handle |
| 6. awaken | 7. shelter | 8. abundant | 9. expose | 10. innocent |

| 1. reasonable | 2. disturb | 3. cautious | 4. Contrary | 5. voluntary |
| 6. fantastic | 7. amazed | 8. primary | 9. occupies | 10. accommodate |

## DAY 9 答案

| 1. conscious | 2. affect | 3. elegance | 4. absorb | 5. interaction |
| 6. celebrate | 7. conventional | 8. distinguish | 9. process | 10. scare |

| 1. documented | 2. aroused | 3. recycle | 4. strengthen | 5. impact |
| 6. formal | 7. professional | 8. potential | 9. regretful | 10. exploit |

## DAY 10 答案

| 1. host | 2. identified | 3. visible | 4. oppose | 5. effective |
| 6. established | 7. residents | 8. manufacture | 9. adequate | 10. vital |

| 1. estimate | 2. affirm | 3. remove | 4. reject | 5. sustain |
| 6. generous | 7. tolerate | 8. stable | 9. display | 10. depressed |

## DAY 11 答案

| 1. overlook | 2. announce | 3. complex | 4. condemned | 5. distributed |
|---|---|---|---|---|
| 6. gradually | 7. novel | 8. desirable | 9. exchange | 10. standard |

| 1. founded | 2. addicted | 3. optional | 4. justify | 5. prejudice |
|---|---|---|---|---|
| 6. distinct | 7. expand | 8. indicates | 9. respond | 10. emerge |

## DAY 12 答案

| 1. withdraw | 2. donate | 3. Regardless | 4. burdensome | 5. instant |
|---|---|---|---|---|
| 6. triumph | 7. preserve | 8. fundamental | 9. represent | 10. fluently |

| 1. reliable | 2. release | 3. neglect | 4. concept | 5. consequence |
|---|---|---|---|---|
| 6. starve | 7. acknowledge | 8. academic | 9. interrupt | 10. deliver |

## DAY 13 答案

| 1. shortage | 2. recruit | 3. accomplish | 4. motivate | 5. budget |
|---|---|---|---|---|
| 6. dedicate | 7. accelerate | 8. productive | 9. seize | 10. enormous |

| 1. rural | 2. capacity | 3. persist | 4. analyze | 5. moderate |
|---|---|---|---|---|
| 6. debate | 7. complicated | 8. entitled | 9. objective | 10. previous |

## DAY 14 答案

| 1. assure | 2. invest | 3. moral | 4. critical | 5. violated |
|---|---|---|---|---|
| 6. survive | 7. temporary | 8. instruct | 9. contrast | 10. considerable |

| 1. appropriate | 2. arrange | 3. crisis | 4. original | 5. surface |
|---|---|---|---|---|
| 6. domestic | 7. intelligent | 8. favorable | 9. interpreted | 10. construction |

## DAY 15 答案

| 1. threaten | 2. survey | 3. passive | 4. harmony | 5. appreciate |
|---|---|---|---|---|
| 6. circumstances | 7. atmosphere | 8. considerate | 9. capable | 10. enthusiastic |

| 1. revenue | 2. reproduce | 3. indifferent | 4. artificial | 5. obstacle |
|---|---|---|---|---|
| 6. mutual | 7. inflation | 8. calculate | 9. emphasizes | 10. capital |

## DAY 16 答案

| 1. credible | 2. religion | 3. trigger | 4. minimal | 5. ensure |
|---|---|---|---|---|
| 6. hesitate | 7. demonstrates | 8. proper | 9. quantity | 10. generate |

| 1. fade | 2. creative | 3. literate | 4. boost | 5. track |
|---|---|---|---|---|
| 6. tackle | 7. campaign | 8. equality | 9. alarming | 10. perspective |

## DAY 17 答案

| 1. exceeded | 2. boast | 3. countless | 4. giants | 5. collective |
|---|---|---|---|---|
| 6. engage | 7. outdated | 8. discipline | 9. accumulate | 10. annual |

| 1. suspect | 2. symptom | 3. implications | 4. contract | 5. casual |
|---|---|---|---|---|
| 6. perceived | 7. slight | 8. attach | 9. definite | 10. principal |

# DAY 18 答案

| 1. enroll | 2. excluded | 3. crash | 4. urgent | 5. translated |
| 6. approved | 7. occur | 8. enforce | 9. fulfill | 10. prosperity |

| 1. liberate | 2. legitimate | 3. enhance | 4. offend | 5. shocking |
| 6. intention | 7. profitable | 8. scarce | 9. conditional | 10. allowance |

# DAY 19 答案

| 1. pursuing | 2. grasp | 3. committing | 4. advocates | 5. dramatic |
| 6. launched | 7. investigate | 8. function | 9. prevailing | 10. combine |

| 1. deserted | 2. boom | 3. heighten | 4. clarity | 5. proclaimed |
| 6. Joint | 7. feedback | 8. Nevertheless | 9. compared | 10. conserve |

# DAY 20 答案

| 1. dispute | 2. obtain | 3. defeated | 4. revive | 5. procedure |
| 6. restrict | 7. discard | 8. reluctant | 9. presence | 10. embrace |

| 1. destructive | 2. monitor | 3. transform | 4. reshaped | 5. decreased |
| 6. champions | 7. bonus | 8. multiple | 9. universal | 10. immense |

# DAY 21 答案

| 1. access | 2. effected | 3. federal | 4. contradicts | 5. operational |
| 6. ease | 7. targeted | 8. massive | 9. screen | 10. accuse |

| 1. disrupted | 2. accustom | 3. illustrate | 4. extensive | 5. outweigh |
|---|---|---|---|---|
| 6. profound | 7. permission | 8. ethical | 9. supervise | 10. collapse |

## DAY 22 答案

| 1. Principles | 2. Numerous | 3. cultivate | 4. response | 5. crucial |
|---|---|---|---|---|
| 6. address | 7. precious | 8. promising | 9. grant | 10. candidates |

| 1. inevitable | 2. distort | 3. renewable | 4. accessible | 5. modify |
|---|---|---|---|---|
| 6. property | 7. impairs | 8. permanent | 9. cater | 10. tend |

## DAY 23 答案

| 1. dismiss | 2. attain | 3. inclined | 4. reveals | 5. content |
|---|---|---|---|---|
| 6. intellectual | 7. interfere | 8. specific | 9. subject | 10. obligation |

| 1. degrade | 2. internal | 3. foresight | 4. scheme | 5. exception |
|---|---|---|---|---|
| 6. pursuit | 7. review | 8. oriented | 9. delete | 10. register |

## DAY 24 答案

| 1. stimulated | 2. witnessed | 3. arrest | 4. endured | 5. provisions |
|---|---|---|---|---|
| 6. navigate | 7. rigid | 8. priority | 9. assumption | 10. licence |

| 1. precise | 2. distract | 3. proportion | 4. assess | 5. confine |
|---|---|---|---|---|
| 6. bound | 7. routine | 8. executive | 9. recession | 10. anticipate |

# DAY 25 答案

| 1. surpass | 2. exert | 3. ancient | 4. relevant | 5. aggressive |
|---|---|---|---|---|
| 6. inhabitants | 7. surrounded | 8. contends | 9. initiative | 10. obesity |

| 1. compulsory | 2. qualify | 3. evaluate | 4. soften | 5. valid |
|---|---|---|---|---|
| 6. lobby | 7. intuitive | 8. terminate | 9. severe | 10. perception |

# DAY 26 答案

| 1. random | 2. conservative | 3. wander | 4. deceptive | 5. chronic |
|---|---|---|---|---|
| 6. evolved | 7. delayed | 8. refute | 9. corporation | 10. logical |

| 1. democratic | 2. vanished | 3. welfare | 4. consistent | 5. shift |
|---|---|---|---|---|
| 6. fuels | 7. exercise | 8. alternative | 9. fashion | 10. tension |

# DAY 27 答案

| 1. remarkable | 2. bias | 3. appeal | 4. outlines | 5. dominate |
|---|---|---|---|---|
| 6. convert | 7. relatively | 8. current | 9. status | 10. gender |

| 1. minimize | 2. upgraded | 3. ambitious | 4. susceptible | 5. sparked |
|---|---|---|---|---|
| 6. Existing | 7. diligent | 8. lessened | 9. vehicles | 10. finance |

# DAY 28 答案

| 1. excessive | 2. devices | 3. ecology | 4. virtue | 5. abstract |
|---|---|---|---|---|
| 6. coordinate | 7. harbor | 8. shrinking | 9. popularize | 10. integrate |

| 1. immune | 2. assume | 3. diminish | 4. widespread | 5. costly |
|---|---|---|---|---|
| 6. charity | 7. rewarding | 8. thrive | 9. initially | 10. subscribe |

## DAY 29 答案

| 1. subsidy | 2. underestimate | 3. highlight | 4. mature | 5. isolated |
|---|---|---|---|---|
| 6. prospect | 7. sacrifice | 8. agency | 9. slimmed | 10. wears |

| 1. prone | 2. imitate | 3. rivals | 4. adventure | 5. skeptical |
|---|---|---|---|---|
| 6. respects | 7. traffic | 8. features | 9. eliminate | 10. modest |

## DAY 30 答案

| 1. grounds | 2. owes | 3. infinite | 4. extinct | 5. strive |
|---|---|---|---|---|
| 6. rational | 7. inferior | 8. collaborate | 9. strategy | 10. correspond |

| 1. participate | 2. alter | 3. guidelines | 4. substitute | 5. fruitful |
|---|---|---|---|---|
| 6. lengthy | 7. absence | 8. disorder | 9. inherent | 10. elite |

## DAY 31 答案

| 1. successive | 2. plausible | 3. counterparts | 4. absurd | 5. constraints |
|---|---|---|---|---|
| 6. infrastructures | 7. contempt | 8. ambiguous | 9. integrity | 10. dilemma |

| 1. squeeze | 2. deprive | 3. opponent | 4. predominant | 5. unparalleled |
|---|---|---|---|---|
| 6. exaggerate | 7. evaporated | 8. assembling | 9. impartial | 10. intricate |

# DAY 32 答案

| 1. intervention | 2. conceives | 3. paradox | 4. insidious | 5. acclaim |
| 6. astonishing | 7. prompted | 8. supplement | 9. vocational | 10. overestimate |

| 1. trivial | 2. curb | 3. resent | 4. reckless | 5. discern |
| 6. frugal | 7. attribute | 8. stagnation | 9. margins | 10. explicit |

# DAY 33 答案

| 1. conceal | 2. impose | 3. vulnerable | 4. accountable | 5. resist |
| 6. aggravate | 7. indispensable | 8. inconceivable | 9. hypothesis | 10. overwhelmed |

| 1. counterbalance | 2. discriminate | 3. privilege | 4. resembles | 5. quota |
| 6. acquisition | 7. speculate | 8. controversial | 9. eligible | 10. mandates |

# DAY 34 答案

| 1. Transient | 2. incentive | 3. identical | 4. transparent | 5. overrule |
| 6. consensus | 7. contemplate | 8. penalty | 9. comply | 10. foreshadow |

| 1. transition | 2. underlined | 3. foster | 4. monopoly | 5. offset |
| 6. looming | 7. disproportionately | 8. overturns | 9. verify | 10. conform |

# DAY 35 答案

| 1. fatal | 2. counteract | 3. aggregate | 4. worship | 5. humiliated |
| 6. compromise | 7. undermined | 8. status quo | 9. liability | 10. scrutinize |

| 1. sponsor | 2. reinforces | 3. uplifting | 4. sanctions | 5. Concrete |
|---|---|---|---|---|
| 6. flawed | 7. conviction | 8. unanimous | 9. intrigued | 10. sarcastic |

## DAY 36 答案

| 1. endorse | 2. facilitate | 3. augment | 4. overshadows | 5. sentiment |
|---|---|---|---|---|
| 6. adhere | 7. obsessed | 8. bizarre | 9. dwarfed | 10. blunder |

| 1. inherit | 2. erase | 3. dearth | 4. embody | 5. zealous |
|---|---|---|---|---|
| 6. implement | 7. onerous | 8. hostile | 9. indulgent | 10. cement |

## DAY 37 答案

| 1. rigorous | 2. demise | 3. heritage | 4. confront | 5. genuine |
|---|---|---|---|---|
| 6. bureaucratic | 7. steady | 8. compliment | 9. scatter | 10. Impressionable |

| 1. cumbersome | 2. distressed | 3. detrimental | 4. drastic | 5. intimidate |
|---|---|---|---|---|
| 6. retrospect | 7. oppressive | 8. disposable | 9. benefactors | 10. geared |

## DAY 38 答案

| 1. suppress | 2. fragile | 3. comprised | 4. grieve | 5. nonsense |
|---|---|---|---|---|
| 6. obscure | 7. incorporate | 8. ironic | 9. extravagant | 10. deliberate |

| 1. infringe | 2. Impulsive | 3. mighty | 4. retreat | 5. impoverish |
|---|---|---|---|---|
| 6. thorny | 7. alleviated | 8. compel | 9. hinder | 10. permeate |

# DAY 39 答案

| 1. backfire | 2. assimilate | 3. transferred | 4. comprehensive | 5. reckon |
|---|---|---|---|---|
| 6. fabricate | 7. yielded | 8. instinctive | 9. induce | 10. aftermath |

| 1. asset | 2. setback | 3. pessimistic | 4. prudent | 5. elaborate |
|---|---|---|---|---|
| 6. intimate | 7. illusory | 8. elevate | 9. deteriorates | 10. fluctuate |

# DAY 40 答案

| 1. devastate | 2. default | 3. eradicate | 4. assert | 5. exclusive |
|---|---|---|---|---|
| 6. resistant | 7. transmit | 8. precede | 9. invalidate | 10. renaissance |

| 1. possessions | 2. Radical | 3. gloom | 4. flourish | 5. peculiar |
|---|---|---|---|---|
| 6. context | 7. cap | 8. refrain | 9. substantial | 10. hierarchical |

# DAY 41 答案

| 1. dispose | 2. assigned | 3. uncover | 4. forecasts | 5. materials |
|---|---|---|---|---|
| 6. instrument | 7. determine | 8. poisonous | 9. instances | 10. counts |

| 1.originate | 2. nutrition | 3. extended | 4. accidental | 5. inquire |
|---|---|---|---|---|
| 6. superficial | 7. derives | 8. expenditure | 9. bankrupt | 10. appointed |

# DAY 42 答案

| 1. creatures | 2. financial | 3. damage | 4. Ordinary | 5. resourceful |
|---|---|---|---|---|
| 6. mindful | 7. regulate | 8. detailed | 9. retain | 10. privacy |

| 1. reputation | 2. characteristic | 3. innovation | 4. worthwhile | 5. cooperate |
|---|---|---|---|---|
| 6. conclusive | 7. tempted | 8. complain | 9. unfamiliar | 10. advance |

## DAY 43 答案

| 1. persuasive | 2. structure | 3. advisable | 4. passionate | 5. weighed |
|---|---|---|---|---|
| 6. overcome | 7. coincidence | 8. landscape | 9. devised | 10. schedule |

| 1. deceive | 2. competent | 3. shields | 4. fortunate | 5. incident |
|---|---|---|---|---|
| 6. enlightened | 7. decorated | 8. relief | 9. switch | 10. insurance |

## DAY 44 答案

| 1. feasible | 2. emphasis | 3. element | 4. boundary | 5. strike |
|---|---|---|---|---|
| 6. literature | 7. contest | 8. divided | 9. belong | 10. explosive |

| 1. consists | 2. unprecedented | 3. ingredients | 4. probe | 5. disruptive |
|---|---|---|---|---|
| 6. clarify | 7. endeavors | 8. framework | 9. slack | 10. thrill |

## DAY 45 答案

| 1. precaution | 2. tighten | 3. reserved | 4. undertakes | 5. momentum |
|---|---|---|---|---|
| 6. respectively | 7. inspect | 8. bothering | 9. circulate | 10. thick |

| 1. tentative | 2. restrain | 3. illuminate | 4. feeble | 5. renders |
|---|---|---|---|---|
| 6. mechanism | 7. eminent | 8. detected | 9. alliance | 10. volatile |

# DAY 46 答案

| 1. durable | 2. withstand | 3. portraits | 4. turnover | 5. dynamic |
|---|---|---|---|---|
| 6. sophisticated | 7. coherent | 8. spontaneous | 9. underlie | 10. threshold |

| 1. external | 2. swinging | 3. overcharge | 4. encountered | 5. characterized |
|---|---|---|---|---|
| 6. boycott | 7. setting | 8. likelihood | 9. constrained | 10. vicious |

# DAY 47 答案

| 1. submit | 2. pledged | 3. intensive | 4. consolidate | 5. harsh |
|---|---|---|---|---|
| 6. reverse | 7. strain | 8. parallel | 9. liberal | 10. neutral |

| 1. foundation | 2. sensible | 3. sharpen | 4. manifest | 5. defensive |
|---|---|---|---|---|
| 6. captive | 7. deficient | 8. exemplify | 9. faint | 10. stereotype |

# DAY 48 答案

| 1. commemorate | 2. appetite | 3. compassionate | 4. censorship | 5. punctual |
|---|---|---|---|---|
| 6. fracture | 7. hospitality | 8. obedient | 9. invasive | 10. ascertain |

| 1. offensive | 2. insulate | 3. prominent | 4. simultaneous | 5. paralyze |
|---|---|---|---|---|
| 6. dreadful | 7. extinguish | 8. instantaneous | 9. propagate | 10. disperse |

# DAY 49 答案

| 1. prosecuted | 2. imminent | 3. capture | 4. striking | 5. brilliance |
|---|---|---|---|---|
| 6. trumpet | 7. institution | 8. arbitrary | 9. corrupt | 10. representative |

| 1. authentic | 2. disposition | 3. miserable | 4. saturated | 5. meddle |
|---|---|---|---|---|
| 6. daunting | 7. proceed | 8. disintegrated | 9. misinterpreted | 10. preaches |

## DAY 50 答案

| 1. nurture | 2. complement | 3. stiff | 4. installed | 5. spectacular |
|---|---|---|---|---|
| 6. magnitude | 7. dubious | 8. anonymous | 9. statistical | 10. monarchy |

| 1. reconcile | 2. substantiate | 3. stern | 4. lucrative | 5. forsakes |
|---|---|---|---|---|
| 6. abdicate | 7. allegiance | 8. litcrally | 9. countermeasures | 10. apprehension |

**图书在版编目(CIP)数据**

考研英语极简刷词手册/徐西坤编著. —北京：中国人民大学出版社，2020.11
ISBN 978-7-300-28737-9

Ⅰ.①考… Ⅱ.①徐… Ⅲ.①英语-词汇-研究生-入学考试-自学参考资料 Ⅳ.①H319.34

中国版本图书馆CIP数据核字（2020）第210423号

**考研英语极简刷词手册**

徐西坤　编著

Kaoyan Yingyu Jijian Shuaci Shouce

---

**出版发行**　中国人民大学出版社
**社　　址**　北京中关村大街31号　　　　　　　　**邮政编码**　100080
**电　　话**　010-62511242（总编室）　　　　　　010-62511770（质管部）
　　　　　　010-82501766（邮购部）　　　　　　010-62514148（门市部）
　　　　　　010-62515195（发行公司）　　　　　　010-62515275（盗版举报）
**网　　址**　http://www.crup.com.cn
**经　　销**　新华书店
**印　　刷**　北京七色印务有限公司
**开　　本**　890mm×1240mm　1/32　　　　　　**版　　次**　2020年11月第1版
**印　　张**　5.5　　　　　　　　　　　　　　　**印　　次**　2024年4月第3次印刷
**字　　数**　125 000　　　　　　　　　　　　　**定　　价**　22.00元

---